BRINGING
TRANSFORMATIVE LEARNING
TO LIFE

BRINGING
TRANSFORMATIVE LEARNING
TO LIFE

Kathleen P. King

KRIEGER PUBLISHING COMPANY
MALABAR, FLORIDA
2005

KH

Original Edition 2005

Printed and Published by
KRIEGER PUBLISHING COMPANY
KRIEGER DRIVE
MALABAR, FLORIDA 32950

FROM A DECLARATION OF PRINCIPLES JOINTLY ADOPTED BY A COMMITTEE OF THE AMERICAN BAR ASSOCIATION AND A COMMITTEE OF PUBLISHERS:
This publication is designed to provide accurate and authoritative information in regard to the subject matter covered. It is sold with the understanding that the publisher is not engaged in rendering legal, accounting, or other professional service. If legal advice or other expert assistance is required, the services of a competent professional person should be sought.

Library of Congress Cataloging-in-Publication Data

King, Kathleen P.

    Bringing transformative learning to life / Kathleen P. King.—Original ed.
       p. cm.
    Includes bibliographical references and index.
    ISBN 1-57524-253-2 (alk. paper)
     1. Adult learning. 2. Adult education. I. Title.

LC5225.L42K54 2005
374—dc22

                           2004042326

10   9   8   7   6   5   4   3   2

2/16/06

DEDICATION

To a vision of new possibilities and all those who stand by us as we navigate the many changes in our lives.

To Chenza, who continues to provide an open hand of freedom, support, and new dreams.

And to my sons, Jim and Bill, that as they enter adulthood they will continually discover their pathways with abundant love and support.

CONTENTS

ACKNOWLEDGMENTS

I acknowledge my professional colleagues who contributed to the development of this book. In particular, several content specialists have assisted in reviewing materials included in this book—Sharon Sanquist, Lisa Wright, and Patricia Lawler. Thank you also to Jim and George for your technical assistance.

I also acknowledge the contributions of the many teachers and learners I have worked with over the years. Thank you for your willingness to embrace my passion for adult learning and for sharing your journey with me.

INTRODUCTION

As we look at the field of practice of adult learning, we sometimes see a mismatch among practice, research, and theory. Because of the marginal nature of adult learning, many adult educators have not had the opportunity to pursue an academic background in the field. Instead, we often only rely on our own experience in the classroom. The aim of this book is to bring transformative learning theory alive through the lives of adult learners and the many contexts in which they grow and learn and to provide adult educators with a basis to extend their own professional understanding and practice. Rather than forcing a theory into practice, the focus is reversed in this book so that through an examination of adults' learning we come to understand transformative learning better.

Based on my experience and consultations with adult educators in many settings, it is apparent that we seek and need the potential of transformative learning brought into the context of our reality, our classrooms. Providing a compelling understanding of transformative learning in the lives of adult learners and its application to the classroom is the major purpose of this book. This explanation builds upon examples from transformative learning in the context of adult education in continuing higher education, English for speakers of other languages (ESOL), adult basic education (ABE), workplace education, and faculty development. The emphasis remains the educator and the learner. Rather than focusing on an in-depth theoretical discussion, this book seeks to answer the question with the adult educator in mind– What does transformative learning mean for my learners and me?

The background of this book is based on my experience of teaching and research in many diverse adult learning settings. For me, academic study was pursued to better understand the teaching and learning I am engaged in, to fill in the gaps, to provide more insight, and to learn new things I could use in the classroom along the way. It is with this same approach that my research has been undertaken: the classroom first and the theory to explain, a focus on learners, and then on how to prepare learning activities that will challenge them. An evolving understanding of transformative learning has motivated me to better teaching and learning, not just theoretical discussion.

Learners' lives illustrate the constantly changing demands they face daily. And the contexts of work and life in the 21st century demonstrate relevance of learning how to cope with this change. Educators and learners describe the hallmarks of transformative learning in significant life and learning experiences that bring them to a place of needing to examine and make sense of their understanding and underlying beliefs, values, and assumptions. They discuss, explore, and test new ideas with others. They continually deliberate about their choices, and sometimes step into new ways of "making meaning" and acting upon their world. These experiences have deep meaning and direction for their learning and their lives as they critically examine and integrate their ways of understanding. Many of them experience comprehensive transformation in their lives. In the words of educational researchers and theorists, these events interweave experience, critical reflection, rational discourse, and action as learners' meaning structures (frames of reference) are radically changed or "transformed" (Mezirow, 1991, 2000; Taylor, 1998).

As the debate about transformative learning theory has evolved over the past 20 years, issues of context, responsibility, social action, and other ways of knowing have been discussed at length (O'Sullivan, Morrell, & O'Connor, 2002; Taylor, 1998). Through its explanation and orientation of transformative learning this book brings the theory and research to the classroom. In the process it navigates these difficult waters of theory through several guiding perspectives. It includes emotion and intellect as it reaches into learners' complex experience to ask questions and seek answers continually. It recognizes the difficulties of transformative educators' responsibility by providing "opportunities" and not dictating transformative learning. It opens the door to social action as learners respond from and examine their communities, but it first focuses on the response and change within the individual. And it does not require a dependency on one way of knowing; the proposed model is designed to be adapted and interpreted to reach multiple orientations, within diverse settings, and for an infinite number of purposes. The book strives to place this basic definition and perspective within a dynamic model that allows transformative learning to flourish within the fertile possibilities of learners' lives. The themes are of expression and expansion rather than confinement to a single interpretation.

When research brings together the excitement of the classroom with the potential for inquiry, amazing results can occur. For me, this has meant seeing transformative learning in action, hearing the stories, seeing the faces, and being part of the creative power and future of adults transforming themselves. This is the excitement and vision I hope to communicate – the heart of what transformative learning means for learners and teachers.

THE POINT: TRANSFORMATIVE LEARNING WITHIN THE LIVES OF LEARNERS

At the center of this book also lies a potentially transformative learning experience for educators – I hope that readers will critically evaluate and construct new possibilities, new dimensions, and a new vision of how an adult learning theory can help to explain and facilitate learning experiences. Individual readers will bring their unique perspectives and experiences to these pages. Never meant to limit practice, the underscoring theme is one of freedom, autonomy, potential, and vision. This freedom is demonstrated in a model that supports designing learning opportunities that effectively and powerfully mesh learner needs, active learning, and the construction of new possibilities - the Transformative Learning Opportunities Model. Adult learners give us the vision of what constructing a future is all about. They give life to the meaning of human potential as day after day they grasp hold of, reach into, and construct their futures. As educators of adults we stand on the sidelines, provide support, lay out possible strategies, and watch with amazement as learners construct their interpretations and realities. Truly, adult learners bring transformative learning to life.

Growing from the stories and accounts of adult learners, a comprehensive approach to planning for transformative learning opportunities emerges that includes planning, delivery, evaluation, and further development. The text stays close to the classroom as it provides scenarios, discussions, and materials for transformative learning across several contexts. Grounded in research that has continued since 1996, comparisons and distinctions can be made across these transformative learning experiences. Using the model gives educators a perspective that reveals similarities and differences of experiences, provides a framework for application, and offers direction for academic and action research.

Emerging from understanding the experiences of learners, this perspective of developing transformative learning opportunities is possible because educators take on the role of facilitators and adult learners become the primary players in bringing transformative learning to life.

THE PLAN: OVERVIEW OF THE BOOK

The first three chapters of the book present transformative learning and a model by which to conceptualize and apply it to classroom settings. The five contexts — continuing higher education, ESOL, ABE, workplace education, and faculty development — are described and transformative learning is illustrated in each. By focusing on the changes experienced by the adult learners, the presentation addresses the needs and concerns of practitioners. The next three chapters discuss the guiding principles for adult educators, and adult education programs by (1) presenting ways for teachers to think about and act on their own assessment of their teaching and of their learners' needs; (2) discussing how adult educators and programs support teachers and learners engaged in transformative learning; and (3) closing with a discussion of the implications for this model and practice for research and development in adult learning, program planning, and professional development of educators. Appendix A contains the Transformative Opportunities Learning Model for easy reference. The other appendixes include classroom materials for each of the areas addressed.

Chapter 1, "Pathways of Transformative Learning," describes transformative learning in the form of several case stories. As with most of the case stories and scenarios in the book, these include composite experiences drawn from research I have conducted over the years, yet presented in such a way as not to reveal individuals' identities (King, 1997, 2000, 2002, 2003a; 2004a, 2004b; King, Bennett, Perrera & Matewa, 2003; King & Wright, 2003). Significant questions answered in this chapter include: What is transformative learning? What does it mean for adult learners? What does it mean for the classroom? And why is it important for me as an adult educator? Chapter 2, "The Transformative Learning Opportunities Model's Guiding Frame," provides a plan for how to conceptualize, plan for, and facilitate transformative learning opportunities.

The following chapters (3 through 6) demonstrate how this model is contextualized in practice. The third chapter, "The Transformative

Learning Opportunities Model in Action," presents the needs of adult educators in each of the specified settings through specific examples of transformative learning. This goal is accomplished through a scenario and description of that setting, descriptions of learners' and educators' needs, a general perspective of adult learning as transformative learning opportunities, and examples of general teaching strategies to support that view. Within continuing higher education classrooms, professors have specific challenges and opportunities for transformative learning as they work with adults returning to higher education later in life in many different content areas. The adult ESOL classroom necessitates understanding the challenges of working with adults with diverse educational, professional, and cultural backgrounds and is often dominated by future test performance. ABE instructors face the intense pressure of standardized testing as the assessment of learner achievement as their work is closely linked to Test of Adult Basic Education (TABE) and General Educational Development (GED) testing and transformative learning may bring the multidimensional needs of adult learners to the forefront (King & Wright, 2003). Trainers have to cope with meeting urgent performance needs and this discussion proposes building transformative learning opportunities that also address traditional workplace expectations for mutual gain. Faculty development, the fifth specified setting, may be seen as specialized professional education cast within the culture and climate of educational organizations, institutions, and schools. Finding new ways to refresh and extend faculty learning can have profound affects on personal and professional development, organizational climates, and teaching and learning experiences. In addition to the discussion and application in this chapter, the appendixes provide classroom materials for each context.

Chapter 4, "For the Educator: The Vital Role of Reflection and Evaluation," presents how reflective practice by adult educators can guide assessment of their teaching and learning. Realizing that transformative learning is not demonstrated in standard assessments, alternative models of assessment for both teachers and learners are presented. In addition, while the transformative learning literature traditionally focuses on epistemological changes within the individual, such learning also impacts emotions, relationships, decisions, and actions in the lives of adult learners and such outcomes are also considered. Chapter 5, "For the Learner: Keeping Supports Strong," discusses issues of support and responsibility that arise from transformative learning among adult learners. Various scenarios illustrate characteristic dilemmas and experiences to guide consideration of these and other issues.

The final chapter, "Looking Forward: Imperatives for Action," summarizes the meaning and possibilities of the model for practice in the classroom with a vision of further research and development that extends transformative learning to new applications. This chapter reveals a vision of new possibilities rather than being limited to our current understanding or experience. The Transformative Learning Opportunities Model offers a framing guide and perspective that support the continuing discovery and developing understanding of transformative learning through the experiences of adult educators and learners.

THE POWER: USERS OF THE TEXT

Individually, adult educators will find a comprehensive, but integrated resource that presents theory applied to their practice in many contexts. This book is also a valuable resource for the personal professional development of teachers of adults in each of the areas discussed. Additionally, adult education students and professors will discover a resource in current research and practice in transformative learning. Collectively, the book is a useful foundational text or resource for professional development workshops and classes in teaching strategies, adult learning, transformative learning, and research applications. It is also an auxiliary resource for the professional development of adult educators. Finally, this text is an updated, companion volume to the classic transformative learning titles that have been published over the years (i.e., Cranton, 1994, 1997; Mezirow & Associates, 1990, 2000). Using the text in this way provides a basis for rich dialogue and debate among educators viewing transformative learning in several contexts at once and bringing theory alive.

THE PURPOSE: PHILOSOPHICAL ROOTS

Questions about the philosophical basis of transformative learning help us as educators examine our purposes. Transformative learning has a philosophical foundation of humanistic and constructivist origins which emphasize the goal of adult learners building and growing into their greatest potential (Merriam & Caffarella, 1999). Yet at the same time there have been efforts to reconcile it with Freire, radical educational philosophy, and other educational perspectives that include social action and critique as the major focus of teaching and learning (Baumgartner, 2001; Elias& Merriam, 1995; King, 2004a, 2004b; O'Sullivan, Morrell, & O'Connor, 2002). This contrasting focus on the individual versus society opens many questions for consideration. But from the practitioner's standpoint, an essential question is, What is my purpose in developing transformative learning opportunities? We as adult educators need to individually examine this question and determine our positions (Wiessner & Mezirow, 2000). From my stance, I see transformative learning as opening up a world of opportunities for adult learners and yet I would never propose to pressure or force learners into change and transformation. Instead, I see transformative learning opportunities as doorways that some individuals enter looking for a better understanding of themselves and their world. Such learning opportunities can provide a basis for lifelong learning by learners critically evaluating diverse perspectives and synthesizing a personal understanding (Mezirow, 1997).

Indeed, transformative learning can be both an exhilarating and difficult pathway. All transformative learning is not rose-colored. Indeed, in some situations there are distressing and difficult choices individuals must face alone; only they, individually, can make the hard choices entailed in truly reintegrating new perspective meanings into their lives. Students may begin to look at their country and culture from a global perspective and ask difficult questions about human rights and political freedom. A middle-aged woman may awaken her intellectual side to discover abilities and potential she did not know existed. They all have to face what they are to do with their prior beliefs, how to handle them, and where to go next. For some it entails intensive dialogue, growing understanding, and stepping into new worlds with those they have traveled with before. For other learners, it includes leaving behind those with whom they have shared life, but who refuse to accompany them into new worlds of exploration. In these ways it becomes apparent that the very context in which learners live is an essential element of their learning experience (Clark & Wilson, 1991; O'Sullivan, Morrell, & O'Connor, 2002; Taylor, 1998). Transformative learning often includes a "growing out of" past world views much like a youngster grows out of last year's clothes. They no longer fit; they pull and bind; they stiffen movement and feel awful. Like such ill-fitting clothes, transformative learning may be uncomfortable and can be a disruptive experience that is not always an "easy" fit.

How can we in good conscience force others to potentially disrupt their lives? I believe we in fact have no business doing so and so do some other adult educators (Magro, 2002). Instead this book lays forth a means by which we as adult educators may do the following:

- Create potentially transformative learning opportunities.
- Provide experience with critical evaluation of one's beliefs, values, and assumptions in a safe environment.
- Introduce coping skills and resources that can help adults if they choose such a path.

From a humanistic philosophy stance, these are vital skills to provide adult learners with valuable choices to face their daily lives and construct their futures. Transformative learning opportunities are building blocks for the future. They provide opportunities to consider, reflect, and choose new paths. They can be open doorways and safe havens for exploration. The choice to take a path of transformative learning is left to learners; we as educators need always to respect and support their decisions

In my ethical framework and cultural context, adult educators cannot responsibly decide to transform learners. These decisions must be left in the hands of the individual learner. Equally important, potential transformative learning opportunities must be cast in a manner and environment that truly leaves open options and does not predispose or force learners into specific choices. Here is a challenge for us adult educators: to envision the possibilities, to lay open the opportunities, and yet to respect learners so that the choices can be genuinely their own. Whether learners choose to stay in current perspectives or reach into new ones, the decision should not be predestined or programmed. Adult learners must be respected, cultivated, and supported to make their own decisions.

Transformative learning pursued from a humanistic perspective is one of possibilities. And the adult educator is a change agent in the sense of setting the scene. If one adopts a radical perspective, then the adult educator, change agent, becomes a protagonist of choices. This perspective fits those from the radical perspective, but this proposal is presented in full knowledge that not all adult educators engender social activism and change. Instead, transformative learning opportunities reveal new possibilities, lay a foundation for more choices for adult learners, and provide coping mechanisms and strategies to develop more inclusive, expansive, and open-ended understandings.

Coming from a more closed, fundamentalist culture at one time, I also understand that a more inclusive view of the world is not welcomed by all groups or individuals. Yet at the same time, looking at our taxonomies of learning, this framework is not one of cultural choice so much as cognitive analysis. Opening new worlds can come at great cost; for this reason, these choices must be left to the individual. At the same time that ethically we do not want to force or influence our choices, preferences, and perspectives on our learners, we are always in a sense culture- or self-bound. We critically evaluate our values, beliefs, lives, and perspectives, but in reality can we ever step beyond ourselves entirely? In fact, cannot this critical orientation become a constricting philosophy and culture in itself? The perspective of transformative learning opportunities presented in this volume can be a seed of a concept that can help us to create learning opportunities for adults in which they can explore and construct themselves and their futures for their purposes and design. Never limited by our boundaries of existence and understanding, I believe transformative learning opportunities offer much more for the adult learner. I see these learning experiences as doorways into new pathways of possibilities where learners are authors, artists, and leaders of their own futures. For truly, adult learners bring transformative learning to life.

THE AUTHOR

Kathleen P. King has been involved in the field of adult education since 1978. She has planned, designed, conducted, and researched adult education programs and adult learning in many settings including adult basic education, continuing education, higher education, technology education, professional development of teachers and professors, and religious education in higher education institutions, organizations, and corporations. King has served on several national committees, including the executive committee of the Commission of Professors of Adult Education, and president of the New York Association of Continuing and Community Education. She is author of *A Guide to Perspective Transformation and Learning Activities: The Learning Activities Survey* (1998), coauthor with Patricia A. Lawler of *Planning for Effective Faculty Development: Using Adult Learning Strategies (2000),* and author of a two-volume series: *Keeping Pace with Technology: Educational Technology that Transforms* (2002, 2003a). In addition, King is founding editor of the adult education journal, *Perspectives: The New York Journal of Adult Learning,* and coeditor of a *New Directions for Adult and Continuing Education* issue, *New Perspectives on Designing and Implementing Professional Development of Teachers of Adults.*

King is a professor, director of the M.S. in Adult Education and Human Resource Development, and director of the Regional Educational Technology Center at Fordham University in New York. She has also taught at Widener University, Holy Family College, and the Pennsylvania Institute of Technology. King received her Ed.D. from Widener University, Chester, Pennsylvania. She also has an M.Ed. in Adult Education from Widener, an M.A. from Columbia International, and a B.A. from Brown University.

CHAPTER 1

Pathways of Transformative Learning

If you are an adult educator who is engaged in the classroom day by day, what is it you think of when you consider adult learning? Many educators tell me it is the faces of their adult learners, which come to mind. For myself, when I think about transformative learning, I envision the faces and lives of learners whom I have known. I think of Isabel who conquered her learning disability and self-doubts in earning a degree, Larry who through careful self-examination and deliberation took the risk of reaching for radically new goals and career, or the countless adults who brave coming to a new world and need to learn a new language and host culture. Their stories in this chapter will illuminate the meaning of transformative learning.

These are adult learners who exemplify the courage it takes to bring their learning into their inner lives. They are the stories we educators often remember, the dramatic transformations and victories that can be part of adult learning stories and illustrate transformative learning. But beyond the exemplars, what does transformative learning look like in our classrooms? Do we understand what it means for our learners? Are we providing experiences that can lead to transformative learning? These are the purposes of this book – to bring transformative learning to life through the lives of adults and to draw our understanding of this learning theory alongside our classroom practice. Through the lives of adults, maybe much like the ones with whom you work, this chapter introduces the pathways and possible meanings of transformative learning for our learners and classrooms

PATHWAYS OF INNER CHANGE AND OUTWARD TRANSFORMATIONS

In many ways we can see that adult learning is a lifelong journey. As you may have experienced when you work with adult learners, facilitating a small part of that learning journey can be a dynamic experience for everyone involved.

One of the things that is so rewarding about working with adult learners is not only building substantial advances in the particular knowledge base under study, but also observing related developmental changes in self-understanding and their own fundamental, "ways of knowing" (Belenky, Clinchy, Goldberger, & Tarule,1996; Belenky & Stanton, 2000; Dirkx, 1997). As adult learners engage in learning new content, skills, and concepts, they also have the opportunity to understand themselves and their worlds in new ways. As we venture forth from our familiar areas of knowledge, we open the doorway to new perspectives and possibilities. Transformative learning, which includes this learning, analysis, and discovery, is one possible pathway along which such experiences proceed. More than a change in specific knowledge or beliefs, instead a new framework for understanding their lives emerges (King, 2004a; O'Sullivan, Morrell, & O'Connor, 2002; Taylor, 1998). It is as if within the mind's eye, the door opens, and learners decide to pursue new understandings and pioneer new pathways for themselves.

Transformative learning's essential elements of critical reflection, dialogue, and questioning beliefs, values, and assumptions, lead to dramatic changes in learners' lives as they explore new ways of understanding and reach toward new possibilities. This questioning is embedded in experience, either primary personal experience that sets the scene for immediate learning, or past experience that is brought out into the open for personal and shared examination. The context of individuals' lives is the beginning and ending of transformative learning in many senses, because learners' understanding emerges from it and they ultimately will have to make their "solutions" work there. Consequently, the classroom experience is only part of the transformative learning experience. What this book's model proposes is that through our classrooms we can build on life experience to create transformative learning opportunities. Herein it appears that most learners may experience some specific elements of transformative learning, and that it proceeds from and extends beyond the space and time of a specific educational encounter.

This journey of transformative learning is not usually strictly linear; it may have many twists, turns, stops, delays, and even re-routing along the way (King, 2002, 2003a). The full details and impact of the "end point" or "destination" are not always clearly defined, and in many respects all of life is one mammoth journey and many micro-journeys at the same time. Educators can be companions along the journey in so far as being a resource, a friendly ear, or a supportive voice (Daloz, 1999; Mezirow, 1997; Pilling-Cormick, 1997). A starting point and/or preliminary course may be fashioned by an adult educator, but ultimately the decisions rest with the travelers, the adult learners. The remainder of the process tends to be primarily under the direction of learners in a self-directed model. Adult learning is a lifelong journey and transformative learning is a possible pathway learners may take at various times during that experience.

In this chapter, a vision of transformative learning is developed in the context of the lives of adult learners. The theory is explained by building on the experiences of learners in many settings, because as we consider the depths of transformative learning, we can most appropriately do so within the lives of our learners. How does transformative learning fit into the scope of the adult education classroom? And how can we as educators benefit from understanding it? In answering these questions the needs and benefits are laid forth, and to complement this rationale, the foundational concepts of transformative learning are illustrated and discussed as to how they relate to several different adult learning settings. Written in the context of our work, our learners demonstrate the meaning of the theory for their education, work, and lives, and provide a perspective of teaching and learning that offers new possibilities for everyone.

Learning from Our Learners

Adult learning is more than academic theory and research; it is fundamentally rooted in the lives and experiences of our increasingly diverse adult learners. We can be reminded of this fact as we reflect on those learners with whom we have worked over the years — remembering the stories of these learners, how they met the challenges they faced, how they came to deeper understandings and appreciation of themselves, and how they reached deeply within themselves and proactively created a vision of new possibilities. These perceptions are at the core of adult education practice built on a humanistic educational philosophy and the basis from which the theory and research of transformative learning have developed. However aside from pure theoretical debate, in considering how adults learn, and focusing on adult learning theory, we also build a foundation to better comprehend and address the needs of the learners with whom we will work today and tomorrow.

In contemplating the lives of adult learners, we would do well to

reach beyond familiar convention. Expanding our vision of adult learning to include many contexts illustrates how widespread lifelong learning is. Not confined to adult literacy, GED preparation, or ESOL classes,
learning in adulthood spans many different environments and purposes.
From the testing emphasis of these examples to the credentials of higher
education and professional certification, adult learning takes place in
formal educational settings. Additionally, informal learning is the context for many adults as they learn on the job, from their experience, and
for recreational or self-fulfilling purposes. In this text, the realm of adult
learning and adult education takes into account many contexts, purposes, and dimensions. The purpose is to see how transformative learning describes some adult learning experiences and how the educator may
develop and facilitate transformative learning opportunities. Certainly
not dictating the direction or choices to any learner, the adult educator
stands ready to support the chosen journey. Adult education becomes
the development and facilitation of learning opportunities that present
learners with safe environments in which to actively consider and reflect
on their current understandings and determine their future direction.
Transformative learning is about the *lives* of our many adult learners
and comes to life in their stories.

Isabel

*Isabel is a 36-year-old black Jamaican woman with four children.
She has been on public assistance for a number of years and has never
completed any educational program. Although Isabel has come into the
adult education program, she believes that she has a learning disability
and that obtaining a high school diploma is impossible. She is caught in
the middle between the demanding employment requirements for sus-
taining full-time work and a lack of self-efficacy and personal achievement. As she enters the program, she continues to work part-time which
serves as another obstacle for learning because it forces her to miss one
day of class every week. Nonetheless, in spite of these difficulties, her goal
is to enter the External Diploma Program (EDP). Entrance requirements
include a minimum score of an eighth grade level in both reading and
math; when she enters the preparatory program, she is at a sixth grade
level in both subjects.*

*Isabel participates in classes and further develops her skills to
qualify for entrance into the EDP program. There she collects community
information and completes weekly assignments that focus on reading,
writing, and math skills. Her confidence increases as she becomes in-*

creasingly proficient in academic studies. Soon she is asked to be an un-official teacher's assistant and this responsibility bolsters her self-confi-dence even more. Isabel experiences tangible outcomes of this self-confidence beyond the classroom as she becomes increasingly capable of resolving problems in other parts of her life. For example, her partici-pation in her children's school life increases and her skills in parenting and communication improve as well. As her skills increase, Isabel be-comes empowered to take greater control of her life. In fact, her descrip-tion of herself becomes that of an active, self-directed, and independent learner who no longer needs the teacher to steer the way. She becomes the protagonist who pursues learning and solutions in an open-ended, more inclusive frame of reference; she develops a new way of understanding and interacting with her world. As Isabel's attitude toward and under-standing of education and learning change, she completes the program, finds a job, no longer needs public assistance, and faces life from a very different point. She captures a new future for herself, creating a new path-way in her life journey.

This experience is one of transformation. A vision of a new way of conceptualizing and interacting with the world emanates from this story as Isabel exercises the newfound self-confidence to actively confront the challenges and difficulties of her daily life. Educational experiences trans-late into not only academic achievement, but also a new way of making meaning of the challenges which surround her. Rather than allowing this dilemma to usurp her goals, she actively undertakes to navigate it and develop the needed skills to fulfill her responsibilities and goals. It may be expected that the same strategies that have helped her success-fully navigate these life experiences will prove successful in coping with additional changes and challenges she faces in the future. From percep-tions of a personal learning disability to achievement of self-directed goals, Isabel demonstrates one example of how inner transformation may be seen in the lives of adult learners (King & Wright, 2003). Next we will consider a broader landscape of personal and professional learning.

How Does Transformative Learning Fit into the Experience of Adults?

In our increasingly global- and technology-driven society, a tidal wave of change constantly engulfs adult learners. On a macro level, eco-nomic conditions, labor forecasts, and international political dynamics are all relentlessly changing. Adult learners who are going to succeed in their studies and life work need lifelong skills to help them cope with the rapid and incessant changes in technology skills, greater performance expectations, and changing responsibilities. These changes will not cease. The same relentless current that churns the waters of national and international change impacts adults day after day, and becoming autonomous learners and decision makers assists in coping with this (Kegan, 1994; Mezirow, 1997; O'Sullivan et al., 2002).

Transformative learning's framework has at its core the dynamic process that learners experience as they gain new discernment and knowledge, wrestle with its meaning, and determine how to reintegrate their learning and insight into their existing, and changing, perspectives (Mezirow, 1997). This theory has gained great prominence in the adult education literature, much like Knowle's andragogy was the cornerstone of adult education for many years. Some would say that transformative learning, therefore, could move into such a central role (Merriam & Caffarella, 1999; Mezirow, 1997; O'Sullivan, et al., 2002; Taylor, 2000a, 2000b). A critical question becomes, What does transformative learning mean for our learners?

At the center of this definition of transformative learning is the process of meaning-making that adults navigate as they critically reflect on their values, beliefs, and assumptions and consider fundamentally new orientations of understanding their world. At the same time this perspective agrees with O'Sullivan et al., (2002) when they say that "transformative learning involves experiencing a deep, structural shift in the basic premises of thought, feelings, and action. It is a shift of consciousness that dramatically and permanently alters our way of being in the world." (p. xvii). This is adult learning that probes meaning and experience and results in life change.

In philosophical terms transformative learning deals with the questions of being and meaning, the epistemology, of the learner. As Kegan (2000) so aptly states, it is not so much *what* we know as *how* we know it when we consider transformative learning. The *processes* of learning and the development of new frames of reference/meaning perspectives are recognized as learning in and of themselves. When learners experience transformative learning and become familiar with the lifelong learning skills related to it, they appropriate new ways to deal with the constant change within which they live daily (Kegan, 1994; Mezirow, 2000).

Larry

This is the experience of Larry who is learning how to use the Internet in his night class - Introductory Computer Applications. Larry first overcomes his awkwardness with a mouse and the multiple demands on his attention while on the Internet through popup screens, cascading windows, and sound effects. He then starts to "listen" to the conversation on a web-based bulletin board and to "talk" about common interests with people from around the world. He has found one group of people particularly interested in photography and is discussing his hobby, daily life, and world news. Larry begins to think of his world in terms much larger than himself, his family, and local community, now considers decisions and issues from different perspectives, and begins to put together alternative meanings and understandings. Within this virtual community of photography hobbyists and professionals, he feels safe enough to test out this way of thinking and understanding and then starts to talk about them with his classmates.

Over several months, Larry gains confidence and begins to expand these individual views into a new frame of understanding. Rather than being limited to his local experience, he develops broader interpretations and orientations. Through these learning experiences, he finds a group of people on the Internet with whom he feels comfortable exploring these ideas and eventually he decides he wants to incorporate his new understandings within his daily life of work and family. These new ways result in new patterns of behavior and new choices which have surprised those around him. But Larry has already tried out his new ideas on the Internet and is reintegrating his newly developed perspective into his life.

Down the road, Larry eventually decides he wants to invest his life in what he finds most enjoyable and meaningful. He decides to leave his desk job and open a photography franchise store. These weighty decisions have many ramifications, and Larry approaches them from the "inside." Working through changing perspectives, he discovers what he really values and wants. Having a platform and community where he can test new ways of thinking and acting provides a basis for stepping forward in his daily life and making difficult decisions. Starting with a continuing education class, facilitated by dialogue and relationships, and built on his own purposes, Larry experiences a transformation in three major areas of his life: his frame of reference, his way of making meaning of his daily life and purposes, and his career goals and decisions.

Learning for the Inside

Isabel and Larry are examples of learners who experienced trans-formative learning in very different contexts and with different results. They engaged in adult learning at different points in their lifetimes and in these instances experienced a fundamental shift in their frame of reference. Their prior beliefs, values, and assumptions were tested and the result has been a substantial change in their way of making meaning of their worlds. Sometimes people who experience transformative learning make dramatic changes in their personal or professional lives. Other times, the change can be primarily experienced within their cognitive inner world. When adults begin to think about their experiences, they may realize they have experienced a profound change. This realization may be at the point of occurrence or it may be 10 days or months or years before they consciously realize it (King, 2002, 2003a).

In the course of our daily lives, we as adults are constantly engaged in lifelong learning. Today more than ever it seems that the pressure is upon us to grasp new information instantly, process its meaning, and make decisions. The press for new skills development is relentless, and the needed rate of adaptation and coping with change has outpaced the past. In the midst of all of this learning, there are times when the changes sink deeply into our understanding and the results become unmistakable. We are changed in substantial ways beyond information, skills, or performance, as the very substance of our being and understanding may be transformed (Cranton, 1994; Mezirow, 1997).

These experiences of transformation may be evident in many parts of our lives, but what is the meaning for the adult in the classroom? Where is it seen? And what does it look like? Coming from forces that push against them from their outside environment and context, adults respond to the need for coping and change. Figure 1.1 illustrates how the outer world may exert impact through economic, political, or other conditions. Closer to the personal life of the learner, the workplace, educational setting, and daily life may encompass challenges. However, the deepest impact is upon the individual's inner being and ways of understanding. Whether this piercing force originates from the workplace or comes through the context of formal educational settings, the inner life and being of the adult, the psychological sense of self, is the focus of this transformative learning.

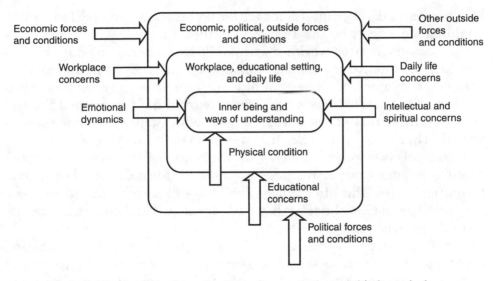

Figure 1.1. Relationship of outside forces to the adult's inner being.

HOW DOES TRANSFORMATIVE LEARNING FIT IN THE ADULT EDUCATION CLASSROOM?

Classroom learning that starts learners thinking about worldviews and perspectives different than their own opens the way for far-reaching change in the personal, professional, social, and work realms of life. Transformative learning deepens the adult learning experience and extends far beyond the formal, classroom experience. By examining other views and learning about themselves, the way they understand, and their habits of mind, adult learners build skills and perspectives that enable them to process and grow from new information, perceptions, and viewpoints and develop new ways of understanding their world (Mezirow, 1997). The stories of transformation tend to be the "big" stories of dramatic changes, but sometimes transformative changes are not visible in the classroom or in view of the educator. Sometimes the changes have an effect on other aspects of individuals' lives. Nonetheless, the impact on learners' lives can be "success" in important ways. Isabel is an example of how self-confidence in the classroom translates into concrete outcomes in family, work, and school. Laying the groundwork for greater independence in learning, skills to continue learning, and confidence to expand one's horizons are examples of powerful changes experienced through transformative learning (Mezirow, 1991, 2000). Transformative learning can take our classrooms far beyond their customary four walls, enabling learners to be the architects of their future.

As an educator working with adult learners day by day, when I consider perspective transformation, it is the faces of the adult learners that come to mind. My research of transformative learning has taken me to a variety of settings where adults learn. I have examined the stories of adult learners in continuing higher education, English for speakers of other languages (ESOL), adult basic education (ABE), and professional development. I have listened to learners tell what facilitated these experiences, but more powerful have been the accounts of the transformation itself. The life changes they have experienced and the new perspectives and life changes they have developed and chosen are transformations to be remembered.

For instance, in my research I have seen continuing education students who return to school to study the career they aspire to and during the process they begin to see the full picture of that career, what it really is, and what perspective or way of knowing is predominate in their field (King, 1997). Sometimes the students continue on excited by what they have found; other times they realize the true delineation of the career is not what they desire and they move on to another career choice. Changing understandings, having new visions, and discovering new ways to live and work – these are examples of the transformative learning experience.

Some adults who enter into the educational process realize a reawakening of their intellectual side. They engage in critical reflection of their beliefs, values, and assumptions and begin to discover new perspectives. As they reflect on their purposes and futures, they may also gain confidence in their abilities and from this confidence be empowered. Seen in many contexts, learners engaged in continuing education, adult ESOL, graduate studies, or professional development may experience such transformational changes (King, 1997, 2000, 2002, 2003a, 2004a; King & Wright, 2003). Transformative learning brings a new orientation and a new focus to learners' lives. The many possibilities that spring from a new worldview can be empowering, and sometimes startling. The literature on transformative learning has begun to describe these transformations as changes in "habits of mind" (Mezirow, 1997, Mezirow & Associates, 2000). This phrase captures the foundational and unconscious way that adults' "ways of knowing" intertwine with their beliefs and assumptions, their understanding of the world, and the decisions they make about new knowledge. When people leave behind a "habit of mind," they find the view of the world significantly different from the vantage point of where they "stood" before. A new frame of reference can bring with it a host of changes that evolve into a new paradigm for making sense of their world on a consistent basis.

Gian

One dramatic example is seen in the life of an adult ESOL learner, Gian, who after several semesters of study at the local college, gains confidence to leave his apartment. He says that before he took classes he was frightened to go out in public because he was afraid people would think he was "stupid" because he did not know English; he was decidedly ashamed and fearful of living in this "foreign" community. He also describes a new way of understanding and learning as he became more active in his learning and empowered to interact with his world in a vastly different way. He has been in the United States 10 years and in ESOL classes 1 year. He relates how, through his classes, he has moved from those many years of fear and shame to confidence and new hope.

This experience was accomplished through a fundamental transformation of Gian's understanding of himself, his understanding of people different from himself, and his assumptions about himself and others. These orientations were fundamentally challenged and reframed to bear a new way of understanding his world. As Mezirow (1997, 2000) would describe, his way of understanding the world became more inclusive, more permeable, and more adaptable through these experiences (Mezirow, 1997). Therein lies the power of transformative learning – fundamental, basic, grounding transformation that serves as a base to generate new frames of reference (Mezirow, 2000), new "habits of mind" (Mezirow, 1997), and new world views (King, 2002, 2003a; Taylor, 1998) for learners to understand their experiences.

What else does the field of adult education know about transformative learning? What are its roots? How is the experience explained and what is included in it? The next section leads us into a consideration of these questions.

THE THEORY AND RESEARCH

Perspective transformation is a process of learning through cognitive, meaning-making, and outward change. Mezirow's (1978) original theory had 10 phases leading from a "disorienting dilemma;" through

critical self-evaluation; exploring of new possibilities for roles, responsibilities, and actions; the provisional testing of new roles; the building of
self-confidence in the new perspectives; and finally reintegrating these
fundamental changes into the learner's lives (Mezirow, 1991). As our
understanding has evolved, we realize that this theory should better
describe a process that is decidedly not lockstep or rigid. Instead, we
should envision an ascending spiral of experience and understanding as
learners progressively experience, reflect, and understand new perspectives of their experience and themselves (Baumgartner, 2001; King, 2002,
2003a).

       There is no target or "preferred" time schedule for this, for as we
know so well, adults process experiences at very different rates and from
infinitely different perspectives (King, 2002, 2003a). The emphasis of
the transformative learning experience instead is on critically examining beliefs that may have been previously unexamined and unquestioned.
This experience also includes developing a frame of reference that is more
inclusive of diverse understandings, perceptions, and even realities.
Transformative learning is an exploration and discovery of meaning-
making for the individual. It has the potential to offer new coping skills
for taking information from the outside world, critically questioning its
value and meaning, and using it to fuel the construction of new constructions or manifestations of knowing and understanding. Transformative learning is learning *for* the inside or as O'Sullivan et al. (2002)
describe, a dramatic shift of consciousness. More than responding to the
demands of the workplace or a qualifying exam, such learning has meaning for changing the conceptualization and framing of our understanding of ourselves (Mezirow, 2000). In fact, it can illuminate our
understanding of ourselves in the context of our worlds. While the transformation may be tied to immediate experience, it is an experience that
can be duplicated many times to different degrees, different purposes,
and different results. It encompasses a dynamic, open-ended, and inter-
pretative learning experience.

       From some orientations, transformative learning is integrally
bound to critical reflection and dialogue. In theory and some research it
is evident that as learners engage in discussing the changes in perspective, considering new possibilities, and exchanging insights, the process
progresses (Cranton, 1994; King, 2002, 2003a). Using the framework
presented by Belenky et al. (1996), one often sees developmental transition from subjective knowing through connected knowing to constructed
knowing that encompasses this experience of transformation learning.

The theory has offered a framework within which to examine this cognitive change, explore its representation and influence on other aspects of adult learners' development and lives, and consider how to facilitate and support it in the educational process (Belenky & Stanton, 2000). Kegan's (2000) phrase, "What form transforms?" is an apt title to help us understand the breadth and depth of this inquiry; rather than procedural, performance-based outcomes, more rooted inner learning, and ways of knowing are at the heart of transformative learning (King 2004a; King & Wright, 2003).

Building on the traditions and insights offered by Dewey and other proponents of experiential learning, transformative learning in one way or another engages learners in exploring their understanding (Mezirow, 1997). When problem solving, simulations, or collaborative inquiry facilitates this understanding, learners have concrete learning experiences that are a basis for critical questioning (Cranton, 1994, 2000) or exploration (O'Sullivan et al., 2002). Such inquiry may emerge from an immediate experience, or one in the past. As Cranton (2001) says, we understand through our experience. Even as different personality types will find meaning through different dimensions of understanding whether it is intuitive, thinking, or feeling, for example, the filter of experience is the one through which most learning needs to reference. Transformative learning may be fostered by engaging learners in active learning that centers about making their own meaning, learning for themselves, and analyzing and synthesizing their perspectives and knowledge (Cranton, 2000).

Constructivism, the educational philosophy in which learners build from experience and construct knowledge and meaning (Fostnot, 1996), is a consistent basis for transformative learning as well (Merriam & Caffarella, 1999). For example, the hum of the collaborative classroom, as learners work together to consider the many approaches to learning and plot a course of inquiry, can be a powerful demonstration of constructivism in learners' lives. Here, learning is not solely the communication or transference of a body of knowledge from teacher to learner. Instead it occurs as the creative result of learner engagement, focus, and construction casts a vision of the proactive potential of adult learning. The excitement of seeing ideas, perspectives, new understandings, and new solutions emerge from and among adults is an exhilarating experience to participate in and support. Adult educators sense that something much greater than themselves is happening during these times. Learners light up, hurriedly explain their insights, and wait to hear how others do or don't understand. There can be an excitement in learning that bursts out from within. Not solely learning for a test, or satisfying requirements, these learners instead break loose from the limitations of workbooks and reach the core of their beings as adults.

LIVING TRANSFORMATIONS

Yolanda

Another way to think about the process of transformative learning is to consider how an individual may experience its different phases. Consider the case of Yolanda, a religious follower who has been raised in a strict home. She is married, and now at age 35 enters college to pursue a teaching career. Within this setting she begins to meet people with very different views about their daily lives, expectations, goals, and responsibilities. She starts to question those beliefs that she has never questioned before and cannot find answers that satisfy her concerns. Even though she is studying education, she finds she is beginning to doubt her personal beliefs quite apart from the focus of her studies. As she thinks about world history, philosophy, and the classroom, she turns her questions within herself to study and test her own and other religious beliefs systems, surreptitiously. Through introspection she considers the possibilities, pursues the logic, and begins to view her belief system in a new way. She develops some new friends in her classes and begins to talk with them about their lives and interests in order to see how her ideas might fit in. Eventually, conversations result in extended dialogue about her core concerns.

Yolanda continues to test and explore, and only after this phase is she comfortable in beginning to bring her new beliefs into her daily home life. One might say that she has put together the pieces of her world in a different order and developed a more inclusive understanding. In this case, Yolanda finds her belief system unbending, so she challenges her "habits of mind" and adopts a new way of making meaning of her world. Her meaning structure — her frame of reference — develops a new pattern and follows a different course from the one she previously held. And this new frame of reference finds expression in a newly reintegrated form in her experience.

As background for understanding, we will look at Mezirow's 10 phases of transformative learning:

1. A disorienting dilemma
2. Self-examination with feelings of guilt or shame
3. A critical assessment of epistemic, socio-cultural, or psychic assumptions
4. Recognition that one's discontent and the process of transformation are shared and that others have negotiated a similar change
5. Exploration of options for new roles, relationships, and actions
6. Planning of a course of action
7. Acquisition of knowledge and skills for implementing one's plans
8. Provisional trying of new roles
9. Building of competence and self-confidence in new roles and relationships
10. A reintegration into one's life on the basis of conditions dictated by one's new perspective. (1991, pp. 168-169)

For Yolanda the "disorienting dilemma" was entering college and meeting adults with different belief systems from her own. As she engaged in her studies, some of the topics included different points of view and philosophies. Yolanda started to think about the meaning of these views and how they compared to her own. But going further, she engaged in the third phase of critically assessing her assumptions about not only her socio-cultural orientation, but also her reason for being (her epistemic beliefs).

As she began to voice her thoughts and test them out with those she had gotten to know in her classes, she found that others had also experienced such questioning and changes. Through this extended dialogue, she tried out new ideas and gradually began to think of herself in a new relationship to her religious beliefs. She reached the conclusion that the belief system was no longer valid for her and wanted to step away from the closed regimen. Yolanda chose to explore possibilities and engage in discussion with her friends, and in these ways tried out the new roles through dialogue and relationships. The most obvious milestone was when she brought together, reintegrated, her new belief system with her daily life and in this case made her difficult choice. The world of school had been another "reality" from her family and religious community. When she gained confidence in her new perspectives and roles, she was ready to take that final step of the transformative learning process into a whole new experience of learning and understanding.

Some people describe the final step as standing at the edge of a cliff, then stepping away from the support of the cliffside, and entering the unknown. While having growing confidence in the new perspective, and having experienced the roles in other settings, individuals face many unknown repercussions when putting their decisions into action in their daily lives. For learners who take the risk, it may be a time of great hesitation and also great courage. It is the courage to engage in learning that reaches deep within their understandings of themselves.

Complexities

Since 1978, the field of adult learning has grappled with multiple meanings, dimensions, and implications of transformative learning. Researchers and theorists have started to explore the affective (King, 2002, 2004a, 2004b), spiritual (Dirkx, 1997; O'Sullivan et al., 2002), ethical (Taylor, 2000b; Wiessner & Mezirow, 2000), natural (O'Sullivan et al., 2002), and collaborative aspects of the theory (King, 2004b; Mezirow & Associates, 2000). It clearly is a theory that addresses complex issues of both adult learning and adult development. While Mezirow's original focus was on the rational and cognitive dimensions of the learning, we now see that there are many more strands of impact to the experience. For example, in studying the experiences of educators learning educational technology, King (2002, 2003a) reveals an emotional progression from fear to exploration to confidence that the teachers experience. The emotional dimension of technical learning is an oxymoron in many worldviews, but transformative learning allows us to consistently support this seemingly unlikely juxtaposition of the rational and emotional in this setting in order to better understand and support adult learners.

Alternatively, Dirkx (1997) and Daloz (1999, 2000) bring forth the consideration of the inner self, or as they designate it, the soul, in transformative learning. The psychological self, the emotional self, and now the inner being are addressed in a theory of learning that grapples with complex individuals and lives.

In addition, O'Sullivan et al.'s (2002) work has brought together diverse voices to explore alternative ways to facilitate and experience transformative learning. These include spiritual, natural, and political dimensions to name a few. Our understanding of this theory of adult learning is burgeoning as we explore its meaning in many contexts.

Transformative learning certainly does not offer easy answers to the challenges of the adult learning classroom; however, it does offer a multidimensional paradigm that can continue to develop with our growing understanding of the learner and the learning process.

Considerations

At the same time that transformative learning holds many possibilities, we as educators need to be aware of the consequences of our actions and purposes. An important distinction in purpose is posed in the carefully chosen phrase used throughout this book - "transformative learning opportunities." Ethically, adult educators need to respect the rights, beliefs, values, and decisions of our adult learners, always (Cranton, 1994, 2000; King 2004a, 2004b; Magro, 2002; Taylor, 2000b; Wiessner & Mezirow, 2000). In providing transformative learning opportunities, we need to delicately balance the value we place on transformative learning and the learner's decision to pursue it, or not. We must be careful and mindful to leave room for the adult learner to say, "I don't want to go there." Adults come to any learning experience with a multitude of individual circumstances and needs. Life in this millennium is complicated. As much as we might communicate the infinite shades of gray that exist in perspectives and understanding, so must we communicate the freedom not to pursue the pathway of questioning and new perspectives. This should not be a value judgment in any way, but perhaps best viewed as our own admission that we do not have all the answers and cannot make decisions for our learners.

In this way, we may also see that transformative learning is an exciting opportunity for us to engage as co-learners with our adult learners: watching them explore meanings and test new understandings, listening to their reasoning and considering their perspectives, and drawing alongside to watch the changing landscape and to sow seeds of contemplation. Transformative learning opportunities have many variations in how they may be experienced and adult educators need never require learners to pursue such changes nor predetermine outcomes. The open-ended experience of transformative learning itself should be the theme of the learning opportunities we craft for our learners. In this way, the individual's strengths, propensities, perspectives, and interests contribute to learning for the inner being. Transformative learning comes to life through learners' unique interpretations for themselves (Cranton, 2000). As educators, we may begin to see this transformation through dialogue and eventually as learners construct their lives through it.

Words that continually come to my mind to describe these experiences include creating, constructing, building, crafting, and painting. Much like a canvas reflects a synthesis of multiple snapshots of an artist's perception, so is the life of the adult learner who experiences transformative learning. Artists start a painting and then may see their subject differently; they in turn refine the image to fit a different view, or even paint it completely over to create an entirely new image. What is put on the canvas emanates from within and metamorphisizes with it as well—so it is with our adult learners also. Educators need to underscore learners' freedom to create that which they are becoming, because it is adult learners who bring transformative learning to life.

WHY DO WE NEED TO UNDERSTAND TRANSFORMATIVE LEARNING?

Our adult learners need to have opportunities to experience transformative learning. As adults encounter fundamental changes in their ways of knowing, their understanding of their world, and their habits of mind, transformative learning provides ways to understand and support them.

Experience with transformative learning builds a basis for lifelong learning (Mezirow, 1997). More than "book learning" and the traditional classroom, transformative learning is that of which life is made. It can encompass adults' development of their professional perspectives and lives; it can include their relationships with family, community, and co-workers. Transformative learning can even describe the development of adults' identities in areas they have not pursued or where they have been unable to go before. This paradigm of learning provides enough depth to include many more dimensions of individuals than we might usually consider. And in doing so it offers power and purpose throughout a lifetime.

Transformative learning opportunities lay the groundwork to cope with changing needs, conditions, and expectations. When the job, school, or economy brings unexpected changes, transformative learning includes a means to critically examine and deconstruct those demands and determine how to sort them out for consideration, action, and/or reframing (Kegan, 1994).

Our framework of transformative learning needs to continue to be open-ended. With neither predetermined results nor timelines, adult educators can introduce their learners to learning skills and perceptions that can take them in new directions. Learners can capture and create their futures under their own power.

HOW CAN WE USE IT?
TRANSFORMATIVE LEARNING APPLIED

As we consider the adult learners we work with daily, it is imperative to consider how transformative learning theory and research may translate into practice. These instructional strategies are effective:

- Focus on learner experiences to determine readiness, recognize history, and validate experience.
- Recognize needs as learners prepare for program entry and as they need support through different stages.
- Engage learners in goal setting as a basis for self-directed learning, using problem solving, critical reflection, and analysis.
- Develop reflective practice (Cranton, 1994, 1997; King, 2002).

Many of us already use instructional strategies consistent with facilitating transformative learning. A pressing question remains as to how curriculum, instructional goals, personal learning plans, and activities can incorporate these purposes and strategies in greater ways. As educators we need to be engaged in thoughtful reflective practice ourselves that leads us into new insights of our learners, their needs, and our roles.

What would a classroom that provides transformative learning opportunities include? What might be happening there? What roles would an educator take in these settings? And how would we design instruction to promote these purposes? Answering these questions is the focus of this book. This chapter offers a brief introduction to some of the solutions the book presents. Overall, rather than dictating specific teaching methods, structures or strategies, I see the solution in terms of a model, the Transformative Learning Opportunities Model. Similar to transformative learning itself, the model is open-ended, depends on the experience and frame of reference of the participant, takes many forms, and holds multiple possibilities. Rather than prescribing any uniform and rigid practice, it includes many choices and independence in building unique learning opportunities for learners to co-create, participate in, and go beyond.

The Classroom

Classrooms that provide transformative learning opportunities take many forms. One of the key elements is that such classrooms have at their center engaging the learner in critical questioning, inquiry, and analysis (Cranton, 1994, 2000). Whether this experience emerges from collaborative inquiry or individualized personal reflection, the emphasis is on considering underlying and overt meaning, process, and knowledge, and using dialogue as a means to better understand them. We push at the edges, checking to see where the limits are, and poking beneath the surface to test whether there is any hidden content and meaning. We might even say that dialogue, whether in real-time, online, or through the pages of a journal or book, is rather like sitting down to the real road test. In whatever ways we accomplish engaging learners in such investigations and conversations, we are starting them along a path of potential transformative learning opportunities.

Such classrooms might have collaborative problem solving in the form of simulations, case studies, or other group projects. Learners may engage in debates, active discussion, or presentations. Students may determine their learning goals, design their own learning contracts, or prepare for certification exams. Whatever the specific forms of activity, the emphasis is on the learners deeply engaging in questioning content, perspectives, and understanding. Once these building blocks are established, learners grapple with incongruities and hidden meaning. Learners may take on the role of those who have different perspectives. They may try on a different frame of meaning, orientation, or social role and explore new possibilities for their understanding and identity. Challenges for learning — whether originating from outside or emerging from within — are at the core of the questioning and debate, internal or external, that learners engage in during transformative learning experiences.

The Educator's Roles

What roles might the educator have in a classroom that provides transformative learning opportunities? As Cranton (2001) communicates, there are as many teaching styles as there are complex personality style possibilities. Certainly our educational philosophy sets the stage for our ways of thinking about, planning, and interacting in the teaching and learning processes. However, as we contemplate transformative learning and how to provide opportunities to experience it, in many of these settings educators take on the role of facilitator at some point. Each of us can probably think of a speaker who turned on the light to a new way of thinking about our world. Perhaps it even was a lecture or public address that was one-sided, delivered from a podium. Nonetheless, for this experience to have impacted us deeply, the speaker struck a chord within us. Something that was said resonated within us and made us think about our purposes and priorities. At such moments, the world can appear to become distorted as it seems out of focus and we struggle to determine the meaning for ourselves. Transformative learning can be experienced when such disorienting dilemmas are the foundation for continued inquiry, questioning, and changing meaning perspectives. In formal adult learning settings, the educator is a likely individual to be a resource, sounding board, or facilitator in many different ways. At various times we might find ourselves challenging our learners to take a thought further, supporting them in their decisions, encouraging them as to the new learning they are gaining, or urging them to reflect on their pathway of learning. Alternatively, one may view educators as composers of sorts as we craft and construct learning opportunities that offer the possibility of, or prelude to, transformative learning experiences.

Instructional Design

As we consider how transformative learning progresses, educators can design learning activities within this construct and with the vital inclusion of adult learners in this creative process:

- Assess needs.
- Consider the affective sides of learning.
- Determine goals and objectives for learning.
- Involve the learner in the planning.
- Create a delivery process that has many points of active learning.
- Accomplish ongoing and final evaluation by teacher and learner both.

This orchestration of teaching and learning can be seen in the use of open-ended activities or a focus on learning as in asking a provocative question that learners try to answer in several ways. Another way that this emphasis can be seen is when we think about learning as discovery and development, rather than as telling information to a passive audience (Pratt, 1998). In planning our learning activities, we have the opportunity to incorporate options and extensions in multiple ways to guide learning experiences. The delivery options will probably involve us in active and dynamic learning, evolving dialogue, and critical reflection. Perhaps focusing on transfer of learning is the most challenging stage of instructional design. However, when we enlarge our vision of learning application to include both tangible and intangible, and the immediate and long term, we can find multiple applications of transformative learning as learners gain skills for a lifetime and develop an open-ended perspective of understanding.

SUMMARY

Transformative learning does not provide a scripted regimen to an all-satisfying solution. Teaching and learning that are learner-centered, open-ended, and dynamic are in fact messy. Ever-evolving, continually generating new ideas, and focusing on the learner — these qualities make the process of learning within a framework that is consistent with transformative learning a challenge for educators. And yet at the same time, guided instructional planning for transformative learning opportunities can tie together the many purposes and contexts of the learning experiences.

With the Transformative Learning Opportunities Model, adult educators aim not to change learners in predetermined ways, but to provide safe environments within which learners can explore their understandings, worlds, and perspectives. By guiding learners to such opportunities, educators can provide experiences that bring transformative learning to life. Learners will be coping with unexpected change, new perspectives, and reevaluation of purposes. By opening up learning to experiences of self-understanding, dialogue, and exploration, transformative learning brings new meaning and possibilities to adult learners and educators alike.

CHAPTER 2

The Transformative Learning Opportunities Model's Guiding Frame

Not meant to confine purposes, actions, or possibilities, the Transformative Learning Opportunities Model is viewed as a framework that can help organize our understanding of transformative learning in ways that guide our preparation and delivery of learning experiences in our many contexts and among our many different adult learners. Given this broad base of application it would be impossible to delineate specific strategies that would apply to every setting, with all learners, all the time. Instead, the model offers a *framework* for the development and facilitation of transformative learning opportunities. Why would we use the model? What are the benefits? Where are the limitations? It is with these questions that we begin the consideration of what the Transformative Learning Opportunities Model can facilitate.

This chapter presents the Transformative Learning Opportunities Model by describing it through three different perspectives of the framework. First, it examines what this model has to offer adult educators and learners. Second, it examines our understanding of transformative learning by presenting the model through concepts, and illustrating it through an extended example. Finally, it describes three dimensions of how educators can use the model to prepare transformative learning opportunities. Targeting the goal of putting our understanding of transformative learning into action, this chapter discusses the model's potential, substance, and use: Why, What, and How.

WHY IS THE MODEL USEFUL?

When considering the needs of adult learning that we face in our many different types of classrooms, we are fully aware that there are no easy answers. However, over the last 20 years adult educators, theorists, and researchers have explored a learning theory that can approach these complexities in several different ways. Several volumes have been writ-

ten that grapple with detailed considerations of the cognitive and rational dimensions of transformative learning (Mezirow & Associates, 1990,
2000). In addition, other publications have aimed to bring the theory to
the point of application and distinguish how we might promote or facilitate transformative learning (Cranton, 1994, 1997). Still, this discussion has focused on facilitation and critical thinking techniques
(Brookfield, 1987; Cranton, 1994).

    In recent years, more research has been conducted about trans-
formative learning (Taylor, 2000a, 2000b), including my own (King, 1997,
2000, 2002, 2003a, 2004a, 2004b; King, Bennett, Perrera, & Matewa,
2003; King & Wright, 2003). By collectively examining some of this research, we can see common themes that describe the teaching and learning processes identified as facilitating transformative learning. A guiding
framework captures some of these patterns and suggests ways to apply
transformative learning to more contexts and groups of learners.

    It is in this vein that the Transformative Learning Opportunities
Model is offered, not as a constraining sequence that prescribes action,
but instead as a framework that reveals new possibilities. The transformative learning frame is distinctly one of constructivism and experiential learning. It incorporates learner needs, engages them as active
learners, and seeks to unleash their energies, insights, and learning to
build new understanding in their content area and of themselves.

    Benefits of using the model include planning for learning that
builds skills and vision for lifelong learning. Rather than restricting learning to a content area, building transformative learning opportunities provides avenues to learn about oneself. Further, it provides a basis to
evaluate oneself, and one's worldview within and beyond a content area.
These dimensions of learning and development are elements of the real
world in which our learners need to survive and succeed (Mezirow, 1997;
King, 2002, 2003a). By building experiences for learners to reflect on
their situation, questions at hand, and their understanding, educators
guide them in exploring and honing strategies for coping with change.

    Some educators might be looking for the sequential elements of
instructional design in the Transformative Learning Opportunities Model.
In fact, the model incorporates and integrates both learners' and educators' experiences and elements. Unlike instructional design methods that
enumerate task and performance analyses to determine a sequence of
learning, the Transformative Learning Opportunities Model incorporates
key elements of traditional instructional design in its guidelines (Dean,
2002; Gagne, Briggs, & Wager, 1992). Indeed, this model addresses con-

cerns that might not be present in other instructional design models. First, the model starts with considerations of building safety and trust in the learning setting. This element may not be seen explicitly, but is embedded within the use of needs assessment. The traditional elements of needs assessment and creating objectives are found in the model's second stage of determining needs and expectations. Additionally, sequencing instruction, method selection, and materials development are all encompassed in the third stage: creating learning experiences. Here not only are these considerations brought into play, but also they highlight the essential elements of critical reflection, dialogue, and application. Finally, traditional design might solely focus on evaluation of the learner. Instead this model embraces the perspective of revisiting needs, teaching, and learning to successfully ascertain how learning progresses and what needs improvement. This evaluation is not solely at the end of the learning experience. Instead, it is used throughout delivery as a way to develop pathways of learning.

Limitations of such a model must also be considered. Any instructional model has the potential of being misunderstood and having its designs misused or abused. For this reason, the themes of learner respect, safety, and participation are not ancillary, but are integral elements in the model. The transformative learning experience poses distinct challenges in its open-ended, evolving, and highly personal interpretations in the lives of each individual. Therefore, the Transformative Learning Opportunities Model is presented with the understanding that it includes and supports these qualities of transformative learning and should be open-ended, flexible, and individually applied. The goal is that the model will be interpreted by each educator, personalized by educators and learners alike, and above all else used to stir our thoughts to how we can plan transformative learning opportunities in our own ways.

Such a model offers a framework from which to embrace these characteristics and blend instructional design and adult learning principles. In thinking about how transformative learning can deeply impact and prepare adult learners, we as educators are continually challenged to examine our values, beliefs, and assumptions about teaching and learning and consider alternative ways to approach our work. This model frames such a viewpoint. By organizing our thoughts with the aid of the framework we can think about the entire teaching process and consider how to incorporate our understanding of transformative learning into each part of it. It provides the opportunity to agree or disagree with the model in part or in whole and the freedom to determine how we as individual educators may best appropriate it for ourselves. The model provides a chance to generate questions and challenges about theory and practice. Finally, the model is a framework, a springboard, from which it is hoped you will launch into your own interpretation within your context and for your learners. While Chapter 3 will present the Transformative Learning Opportunities Model through detailed application in five adult learning settings, the remainder of this chapter presents its guiding framework through illustrations and discussion of its meaning for adult learners and educators.

OVERVIEW

Growing out of research of transformative learning experiences in several settings, this instructional design model offers guidelines for developing transformative learning opportunities (King, 1997, 2000, 2002, 2003a; King & Wright, 2003). Rather than being a script or formula for routine development, it is more a series of considerations that educators address in designing learning experiences for adults with transformative learning in mind. The model draws upon what we know about adult learners and the expectations they have for learning. It incorporates the findings of research across contexts and is built from how learners experience transformative learning in diverse educational contexts. Rather than being a simplistic "recipe for success" it serves as a basis for developing open-ended, individualized, challenging, and stretching learning experiences for adult learners. The Transformative Learning Opportunities Model is designed in two layers of activity: *Layer 1: What does the learner experience?* and *Layer 2: How does the educator prepare?* Additionally, a holistic perspective presents a composite view, which integrates the experiences of the learners and educators. (See Figure 2.1).

Layer 1 of the Transformative Learning Opportunities Model is supported by essential elements of building safety and trust, determining needs and expectations, creating learning experiences, and revisiting needs, teaching, and learning. Both in the experience of the learners and educators these stages are frequently revisited.

In creating the learning experiences educators facilitate learners engaging in exploring their needs, and critically evaluating and explaining their perceptions and insights. As learners share their views of their experiences, values, and beliefs, they may come to know their perspective in new ways. In these experiences, dialogue provides a sounding board and dynamic exchange with others that enables learners to exam-

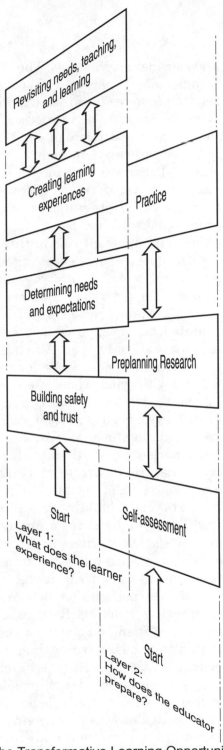

Figure 2.1 The Transformative Learning Opportunities Model.

ine their standing and consider alternatives. The outgrowth of such conversations, whether in person, on paper, or via other means, mean that learning experiences need to move towards envisioning the application of the insights. How would learners' perceptions affect what they think or what they do? Do they see consistency in what they believe and how they act? Do they agree with the assumptions that they have been making their decisions upon? These are examples of questions that underscore the operationalizing of transformative learning into application, action, and choices and need to be integrated in extending and revisiting transformative learning opportunities.

Facilitation plays an important role in this model, as one of the beauties of working with adult learners is that their lives, perspectives, and contexts are multidimensional and always unique combinations. Layer 2 of the model is a guide for us as educators. As we approach our expectations for learning, consider the needs and desires of the learners, craft a plan, and facilitate learning experiences, we need to provide both freedom and guidance for it all to happen. Much like navigating a raft down a swiftly moving river, we need to consider the current, watch out for obstacles, and still enjoy the ride. These many monitoring activities include swift assessment, recovery, and redirection. In the same way, as we work with adult learners we need to provide such direction while also cultivating assessment and monitoring skills. Together, educators and learners need to plan experiences and then evaluate learning expectations and experiences to chart their current and future activities/courses and guide travelers who follow them. Such reflective practice and learning will feed into the next cycle of building transformative learning opportunities so that they never become "standardized," but instead continue to grow with the specific learners, their needs, and contexts.

Figure 2.1 shows the stages interrelating with one another dynamically. This relationship is an important characteristic as information and feedback from the learner/s, educator/s, and process can lead to revisions of prior preparation or action. Returning to the river-rafting analogy, just as we consider changing conditions as we watch the current, so do we consider initial needs, learning progress, additional emerging or changing needs, and assessment alternately while engaged in facilitating such learning experiences. Teaching adult learners in ways that include their critical evaluation of their beliefs, values, and assumptions cannot be done on autopilot. It is an evolving adventure and journey within which we can co-navigate with our learners. The learner's experience is more specifically considered in the next section.

WHAT DOES THE LEARNER EXPERIENCE?

The four stages of the Transformative Learning Opportunities Model, Layer 1 are building safety and trust, determining needs and expectations, creating learning experiences, and revisiting needs, teaching, and learning. This section starts with an example of what the experience may look like in one particular setting — the workplace— and what its meaning might be for an adult learner.

Jamal

Jamal has been a manager with his company 20 years, and now is being mandated to use an entirely new system for his work. No longer will personnel evaluations be completed in checklists and a narrative summary. Instead a new assessment system will be used with new criteria. Prior to this time he would interview staff, dictate his assessment, and have his assistant input it onto the appropriate forms. This familiar format is now obsolete. Information will be gathered on some new basis of performance and goals, and entered into an extensive software program. Performance evaluation and goals will then be automatically generated for an annual review. Later these documents will be used when the employee consults with human resources to update a personal professional development plan.

Fortunately, the human resources department in the company also has a training staff that considers adult learners' needs and seeks to build transformative learning opportunities. Jacqueline is one of the key trainers and talks with Jamal about his needs with this change in policy and implementation. She discusses with him about how he perceives the changes affecting his day-to-day work. Together they explore not only the procedural changes, but also his thoughts and feelings about the changes. She tries to ascertain whether Jamal might be excited, satisfied, frustrated, fearful, or angry about the impending challenges so that she can use the new software's capabilities to design a program of development that will suit him best. Taking the time to listen to Jamal talk about the challenges of the evaluation changes reveals what he needs from human resources, but she also knows it is important to genuinely validate his concerns and attend to the personal side of learning.

Jacqueline asks Jamal what his goals and objectives are and how he best learns new skills and concepts. She also has several topics to suggest across areas including basic technology skills, management, and the specific software package that will be used. Their consultation closes with

Jamal planning to email Jacqueline his thoughts on what his professional development should include. They also schedule a time to discuss the draft of a plan that Jacqueline will construct based on Jamal's input and needs.

At their second meeting, Jacqueline has the draft professional development plan for Jamal that includes the key items that both he and the company have identified. She includes time to learn, reflect, reinforce, and apply what is being learned. Although she ties specific items to time frames, she clarifies with Jamal that these are estimates and that there is time included in the plan to be flexible based on how learning and adjustments are progressing. What seems right? What seems wrong? Does it seem too rushed? Are there items that he does not want to include? Are there any items he does not understand? These are a few of the questions that their conversation covers in the second meeting. Once they revise her proposed plan based on his feedback, they are able to see how he can fit classes into his schedule. Jacqueline and Jamal also plan several times throughout the development plan for them to review his needs and progress, and make any adjustments that may be needed.

Four weeks later, as Jamal heads to his fourth session of classes, he considers what has been happening. He certainly did not expect to be engaged in conversation about his opinions of the software and his ideas about performance assessment. Rather than these classes being "skill and drill" sessions, the students have discussed the concepts as they work through the material. The employees continually interact with the various trainers and one another. Together, they find ways that the new techniques and materials support or need to inform change in their company current structure and policies. They also make recommendations for improvements in the system.

As Jamal sits down in class, Ken, the training supervisor, indicates that they are going to consider how both teaching and learning are progressing. Ken asks them to open the file that has their weekly journal notes and to look for any patterns. How did they feel when they started classes? Why was that? What were their questions at that time? Have they been answered yet? Are there learning experiences they do not fully understand? Do they need more instruction or practice in certain areas? How well are the trainers doing? What are the learners' expectations of the trainers and why? Are the trainers clear about their expectations for the learners? Do they answer their questions fully? Do they seem to understand and provide the support the learners need? What other support do the learners expect?

Jamal and his co-learners write brief responses to these questions, which are collected and merged. In the next session, they discuss the responses and see if they want to change anything about their class. But in addition to formatively guiding and developing the classes, these opportunities for reflection awaken within Jamal a new way of looking at his expectations of teaching and learning and result in his examining his expectations in other areas of his work. He feels great appreciation for how it gives him a new way of understanding his frame of reference and work, and makes him feel more satisfied and understood.

On another level, central to each session is the final action plan that incorporates how they apply what they learn. At the end of each class, the learners use numbered points to plan the steps, time frames, and strategies they use to implement their learning. Jamal finds this awkward at first, but the satisfaction he feels when he reaches his goals creates great anticipation for him as he thinks about participating in the next session.

These classes reach deeper within him than just learning how to use the new materials and computer program. He feels something different and talks to Jacqueline about these ideas and aspirations when they have their periodic meetings. Together they review the training opportunities available through the company and schedule some more, but this time they look at the topics of management styles and skills. Jamal considers where he wants to go next with his career. New options appeal to him and he starts thinking about his satisfaction and fulfillment with his work. Luckily, his company has a lot of possibilities in the career ladder and he identifies some that build upon his new desires and talents that have been revealed through his learning. Jamal can see this is not the end of the road and he is enthusiastic about what future he might create for himself.

Jamal's professional development experience opens the door to potential transformative learning. He is thinking in a new way that is leading him to question his abilities, purposes, and goals. More than critical reflection he stands on the brink of fundamentally shifting his way of understanding and relating to his world.

As adult educators, we work in a myriad of contexts, so the details, flow, and application of the model will be different in each situation. This section will explore the model in terms of the learner's experience and the adult learning knowledge base. Where do the individual elements come from? How do they fit with our understanding of transformative learning? And how do the learners experience them? Carefully considering each stage unfolds the possibilities of the model. See Figure 2.2.

Building Safety and Trust

The essential theme of building safety and trust is foundational for the Transformative Learning Opportunities Model. Different educators use different phrases to communicate this theme, but it is found in the transformative learning literature under the topics of empowering and supporting learners and building a welcoming climate (Brookfield, 1987; Cranton 1994). Underscoring this element is the fact that as learners engage in potentially transformative learning experiences, they risk elements of themselves. These are not purely theoretical discussions; instead learners test and critique their core beliefs, values, and assumptions. For this to be a successful experience, learners need an environment where they can feel their self-esteem and personal value are safe.

Learners can experience safety and trust through discussion and presentation that value individual differences, recognize multiple perspectives and realities, and affirm the individual (Cranton, 1994; Pilling-Cormick, 1997). These core values can be communicated in word, attitude, and environment. Learners can participate in creating such a comfortable environment. Relatively simple modifications and additions such as refreshments, comfortable seating, and adequate ventilation can make big differences. Additionally, learners should share ideas for group guidelines for conduct that might include respecting others' views, giving equal airtime to participants, and preserving confidentiality (Brookfield & Preskill, 1999). Learners can experience safety and trust through facilitation techniques that support participation, contribution, reflection, queries, and conflict resolution. The organizational climate needs to be critically assessed and perhaps modified to provide safety for learners. Realizing that transformative learning is not compartmentalized from other elements of individuals' needs requires that we look at the environment in multiple dimensions — the physical, organizational, and cultural climates, for instance (Mezirow, 2000). Cultural considerations extend beyond a classroom or organization into the personal and social environment in which individuals live. The learning environment needs to be established early on as a welcoming place where people can come to be themselves and be accepted as such. It is from this zone of safety that individuals become more capable of taking the risk to examine their existing frames of understanding and ask the hard questions of themselves.

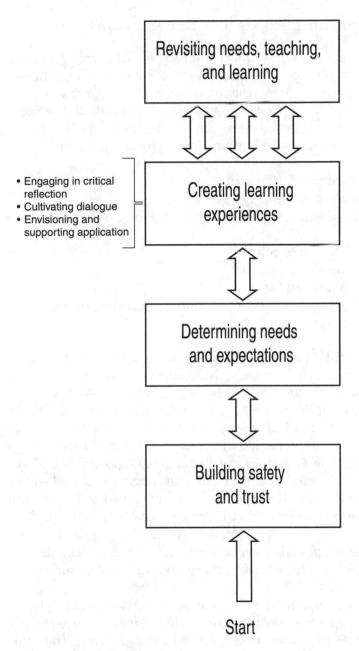

Figure 2.2 The Transformative Learning Opportunities Model, Layer 1: What does the learner experience?

Determining Needs and Expectations

In determining needs and expectations in adult learning, there is a rich literature that includes many different strategies for gathering information about learners and instructional expectations (Cranton, 1987; Dean 2002; King & Jakuta, 2002; Queeney, 1995; Vella, 2002). Learners' needs and expectations might be determined directly or indirectly, depending on the circumstances and environment, by the following:

- Conversing with learners at school.
- Visiting their place of work.
- Contacting them via after-work or evening phone calls, emails, or faxes.
- Reviewing completed curriculum.
- Examining their program records.
- Discussing their expectations.
- Conducting surveys, checklists, and orientation focus groups.
- Utilizing task analysis.

These many options illustrate that needs assessments can be simple or complex, limited or comprehensive, individual or collective. As adult educators in the field have told us before, "Above all else, *use* needs assessment!" (King & Jakuta, 2002, p. 170). Theoretically the educational field is devoted to the importance for needs assessment, but the track record is that in adult education they have at times not been heavily used (Queeney, 1995). The Transformative Learning Opportunities Model is foundationally constructed on the need to ascertain and build upon the needs of the learners and the expectations for the program. Without having this information, we construct learning experiences in the dark and hope that the arrow hits the target. Instead of being in the dark, learners' participation in needs assessments brings light to the process and provides at least an outline for targeting meaningful learning experiences.

Certainly teaching and learning are not always this straightforward. But when prospective learners and stakeholders are involved in talking about needs and expectations, we gain insight from the start into what is needed and whether there are any potential conflicts. How disheartening it is to invest much time and energy on instructional preparation, to only arrive on site and realize you had not anticipated the true needs of those in session with you. How much more powerful it is to involve learners and gather information beforehand, and be able to contemplate, analyze, and ask additional questions to form a basis for a preliminary plan for learning. In my experience, being able to focus on the right target brings more of our quality time and focus to the task. Facilitating transformative learning opportunities is a process that continues blending the several factors until the right combination comes together through implementation. Educator and learner involvement prior to the teaching moment can yield a powerful product that might not come in the flash of the teaching and learning experience alone.

Creating Learning Experiences

As the model progresses, we recognize a new dimension as determining needs and expectations leads to creating learning experiences. The model here is very open-ended and branching. Unlike some other models used to describe instructional design, when planning transformative learning opportunities one must think in terms of multiple pathways of experience.

Learners are starting from different experiences and understandings, and as they participate in transformative learning opportunities these combine in unique ways. Educators play greater or lesser roles, depending on the learners and the situation, in helping them sort out and prioritize their needs and goals. Educators can offer options to learners and have learners engage in constructing their own unique learning experiences based on expectations, time limits, and resources.

This creative process is much like what we could imagine if a small group of people designed a building. Together they discuss and plan; they work toward consensus or bargain alternatives until they have a design. Then together they contribute the different parts of the development and learning experiences so that they can unfold and further evolve through their guidance and participation. You can imagine there is a lot of activity and in some formats it might be quite noisy. Collaboration and collective leadership can be powerful in composing the plan, or blueprint, and guiding the players through the experience.

Within this model, while you have some people working through the same activities, there are also individual differences and therefore you may have many multiple pathways of experience and learning (Cranton, 1997). This dynamic, interactive development feeds back onto itself for revision, further development, and fine-tuning. It involves learners throughout its conceptualization, development, delivery, and assessment. It is loosely coupled, or linked, so participants can reallocate the pieces or assignments and pursue them if it is in their interest and best abilities to do so. In these ways, the model is distinct from many instructional design systems and allows for the experiences of both instructor and learners to be the formative elements in the "building" of their learning experiences. No longer confined to the initial blueprint on the page, these learners craft their own creation, every day, every time they work together to that end.

My hope is that this model can explain in this creative and constructivist design some part of the excitement that learning experiences offer when fueled by the talent of educators and learners working together. In creating learning experiences, three instructional elements are delineated as highly consistent with transformative learning opportunities and often identified through research and theory: engaging in critical reflection, cultivating dialogue, and envisioning and supporting application.

Engaging in Critical Reflection

The roots of transformative learning are found in the critical reflection of the being and self. Indeed, several authors remind us that critical thinking is at the core of transformative learning and the majority of suggestions for facilitating transformative learning come from critical thinking techniques and an emphasis on dialogue (Brookfield, 1987; Cranton, 1994, 1997; Dirkx, 1997; Pilling-Cormick, 1997).

Transformative learning opportunities build on a foundation of safety and trust where learners can ask difficult questions of themselves. Such questioning may take many forms including discussion, debate, simulations, case studies, journal writing, self-assessment, and problem solving to name a few (Brookfield, 1987; Cranton, 1994; Pilling-Cormick, 1997). The essential point for this model is to realize that critical thinking is a vital element and to discover how to cultivate it across a multitude of different experiences (Pilling-Cormick, 1997). How do we help learners identify the questions? How do we encourage critical analysis of learning? How can learners begin to examine their assumptions? As in our preceding scenarios, these lessons can be incorporated subtly and gently into learning when they need to be brought forth. Alternatively they can boldly lead and focus activities when learners are eager for answers to the questions they are already asking of themselves and one another. As educators, we need to develop ways to build in these techniques and experiences when we craft transformative learning opportunities.

Cultivating Dialogue

The element of dialogue is another critical component of creating transformative learning opportunities. Mezirow states over and again the essential nature of this point in describing how we come to understand our assumptions and values; we begin to examine those habits of mind as we engage in discourse one with another (Mezirow, 1997). Dynamic critical discussion needs to incorporate probing meaning, questioning assumptions, and supporting learners all at the same time (Brookfield & Preskill, 1999).

Experienced educators know the power of interesting, deep, and meaningful dialogue among learners. When the fires of learning are lit and people turn to questioning themselves and delving deeper to explain themselves to one another, new power is released and new learning journeys unfold. In experiences like these, learners move forward under their own steam to branch out in new directions of learning: the possibilities and alternatives sometimes come together quickly; growing understanding dawns; and learners begin to see a very different perspective. Not usually a linear process, these experiences sometimes enable learners to build new pathways and constructions that seem to come from nowhere. Dialogue is often the vehicle, directly or indirectly, within which this understanding is revealed. Building opportunities to talk about substantial understanding and learning is essential in the Transformative Learning Opportunities Model and includes many possibilities, for example, face-to-face, online, or asynchronous discussions; simulations; case studies; small or large groups; local or distant participants; insiders or outsiders; and teachers and learners.

Envisioning and Supporting Application

While intellectual exercises are rewarding for many in and of their own right, much more needs to happen for potential transformative learning to filter down into the experience of the learner. As educators we need to consider what our role is in supporting application of learning. If we bring people to the doorway to view new possibilities, do we not have an obligation to support them in some ways if they step forward? And how is this evident in the learning experiences?

Cranton (1994) draws our consideration to these issues as she encourages us to prepare learners to consider the consequences of their decisions, to realize there is adjustment needed, and to explore through dialogue and extension how new perspectives might fit or not. Some educators might think of this as transfer of learning, but in terms of transformative learning it is more than application; it is in fact dynamic, creative action.

Envisioning and supporting application can be accomplished in many different ways including ongoing discussion groups, task-focused groups, role playing, and simulations. Rather than resting sole responsibility on the educator, learners need to participate in developing lifelong learning skills and experiences. Our responsibilities as educators are to set the tone for acceptance; build learning opportunities that invite envisioning goals, pursuing learning, and focusing on application; and support critical evaluation of each individual's own decisions. Again, experiencing transformative learning opportunities is a dynamic coordination of activities.

Revisiting Needs, Teaching, and Learning

As we move out of the intense activity of the prior guidelines, we address the seemingly stiller waters of evaluation. A key point to address up front however is that this evaluation does not begin at the endpoint of the learning process: instead it runs throughout the experience. This approach continuously develops and facilitates the learning activities.

The model builds in ways that educators and learners can revisit and evaluate teaching and learning while it is still underway. Certainly when learning is taking place over a short time span, there may not be many options for evaluating progress and revising the plan. But in longer courses of study, this evaluation significantly charts and informs a pathway of learning that will meet evolving and critically important needs. Information gathered can be used to create highly relevant follow-up sessions and continued learning opportunities.

This model is not one of sterilized procedures; it instead builds upon our experience working with learners in these ways. It is an open-ended model ready to be customized and individualized to the needs and learners that we approach within each learning experience. There are no easy answers here, but there are an infinite number of possibilities waiting for our learners and us to develop.

Here We Go Again!

As we reach the end of the sequence, we have only really just begun. With the bulk of the experience behind us, we must continue to evaluate and to revise our plans. Very often we also will see that out of all the activity, discussion, and learning more questions arise. Together this new information and these new perspectives lead to the identification of additional needs for learning. Within this model, then we lead learners in reviewing how safety and trust can be reinforced, identifying what additional specific needs and objectives might need to be addressed, and building yet more transformative learning opportunities to reach toward the potential of the learners.

One of the characteristics we possess as human beings is the power of the mind to imagine and create. In this same vein, the Transformative Learning Opportunities Model is designed to be a dynamic, open-ended, cyclical, overlapping process that generates more possibilities with each rendition. As adult learners explore the possibilities, new connections are formed and constructed. This is the power of transformative learning to provide fertile ground in which new paradigms of examining the world come alive. With each cycle of these learning experiences, that changing perspective can be questioned and deepened or discarded; the individual makes the choice.

As we educators catch the vision of what transformative learning can be like in our classrooms, and as we begin to further pursue how to build such opportunities for learning, we open new worlds of possibilities. While the human imagination cannot conceive of the full extent of possibilities in the future, transformative learning provides a window into its generative power. The power of transformative learning is found within the adult learner. It is demonstrated when adult learners reach deeply within themselves to bring forth and unfold the future they are constructing for themselves. It is as if educators are the farmers, studying, cultivating, and tending to the field, and the power of life springs from a combination of plants, the adult learner, and the ground, transformative learning. As the cultivation, adult learners, and the learning experiences combine, they build a synergistic creation. Adult learning theory and facilitation techniques on their own are just potential: a way of understanding what can happen. When the potential for substantial learning combines with the lives of adult learners, transformative learning comes to life.

HOW DOES THE EDUCATOR PREPARE?

How do educators who have caught the vision of the transformative learning experience prepare for developing such opportunities? What needs to be done for the learning experiences to develop and proceed? Aside from the perspective of the learner, how does this experience unfold in our work as educators? Layer 2 of the Transformative Learning Opportunities Model and reveals how we can organize the educator's activities for implementation. Remembering that educators within this framework are not scripting or programming learners' behavior, I suggest that we begin with ourselves, consider the forthcoming situation, develop an open-ended and flexible plan, and launch the learning experience. These areas of preparation are self-assessment, preplanning research, and practice, and are illustrated in Figure 2.3.

Self-assessment

One of the best starting points is to begin with ourselves, the educators (Cranton, 1994, 2001). In many ways creating and facilitating transformative learning opportunities is predicated on our own ability to critically evaluate our values, beliefs, and assumptions. Certainly we must examine them in the context of teaching, learning in general, and more specifically, transformative learning. We need to engage in reflective practice and look at ourselves, and consider how and why we teach the way we do. Looking at our expectations and assumptions about teaching, learning, and our learners may take us into areas we do not always have the chance to consider and reflect upon amidst the many demands for our time and energy.

Some of the ways we can engage or structure our self-assessment include keeping a journal, using self-assessment tools, talking with our colleagues, and reading more about teaching and learning among adult learners. Essential to this process is having the freedom to analyze ourselves without ascribing judgmental value to the outcomes. Just as we give our adult learners the freedom to grow and change, and would not judge their starting points and progress, so we must be supportive of ourselves. We are experts in our field, and as experienced educators, we have worked hard to build our practice on our current understanding. Self-assessments should be looked at as opportunities for gains and growth. We raise new options and open new doors of opportunity that will deepen who we are as individuals, educators, and learners. Impor-

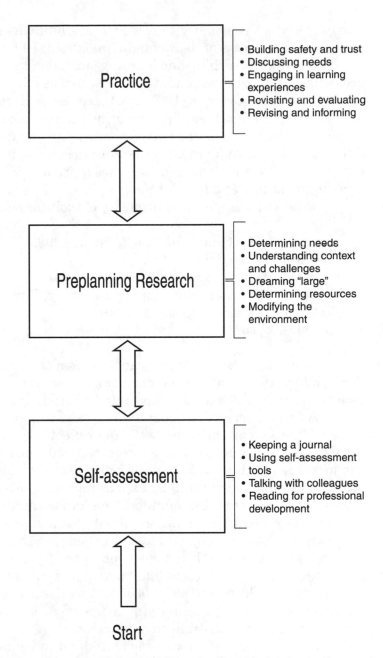

Figure 2.3 The Transformative Learning Opportunities Model, Layer 2: How does the educator prepare?

tantly, we must remember that we too are adult learners and we are always in the process of "becoming" (Brookfield, 1995; Cranton, 2001).

Keeping a teaching and learning journal helps focus on where we are, what it means to us, and what we desire as educators (Apps, 1991; Brookfield, 1995; Cranton, 1997, 2001; Lawler & King, 2000). The self-dialogue that runs across the page brings to our consciousness beliefs, values, and assumptions we may never have articulated before. In addition, a private journal provides safety to express opinions that we may not want to share with others. Here lies a private space for contemplation, appreciation, and possibilities.

Educators can use a multiplicity of tools for self-assessment:

- Teaching styles (Galbraith, 2002; Pratt, 1998).
- Learning styles (Conti, 1998).
- Personality types (Cranton, 2001).
- Values clarification, educational philosophy (Zinn, 2002).
- Technology skills (King, 2002, 2003a).
- Measures of content knowledge (Lawler & King, 2000).

Pursuing these on our own can be a great challenge, but colleagues, through faculty or professional development centers, consortia, and associations, can be sources of support and additional suggestions.

As we reflect on our understanding and engage in discussion with those who are doing the same, we bring reflectivity to a different level. Once identifying others who are interested in discussing their teaching and learning in this way, and laying groundwork of safety and confidentiality, educators learn much by explaining their ideas. By engaging in discourse, we have to refine our ideas, explain them further, think about aspects that we make assumptions about, and ask new questions of ourselves. Such dialogue among trusted colleagues can be an energizing greenhouse for the growth and development of our personal professional understanding. We do well to build a group of colleagues committed to these purposes. Cranton (1994, 2001) further describes several tools and activities and provides guidance in navigating this process in a manner consistent with critically reflective practice.

As educators, when we come to understand our own perspectives on teaching and learning through the lens of our experience and assumptions, recognize this condition, and wrestle with its meaning for ourselves, we are much more ready to facilitate such an experience among and with our learners. In some fields they talk about "earning the right to be heard"; regarding transformative learning it may be a matter of "building a base to understand." In describing the authentic educator, Cranton (2001) reveals the roots of such preparation as entailing an understanding of self as a basis for our understanding and work as educators. Her suggestions for exploring and developing ourselves in these areas are highly valuable in considering our self-assessment. Writers such as Apps (1991), Brookfield (1990, 1995), and Palmer (1998) can be inspirational to fueling self-study that focuses on the "inner life" of the educator.

Preplanning Research

In order for educators to use the Transformative Learning Opportunities Model, it is important to build on this self-assessment and then engage in preplanning research. Major areas addressed in preplanning include determining what needs can be ascertained prior to meeting with the learners, understanding the context and challenges that learners face, dreaming "large," and determining available resources and the environment in which learning will take place.

Prior to making an instructional plan we know that the "correct" steps include conducting a needs assessment. But like many things in life, do we really follow these directions? It is critical here that educators pursue needs assessment, although learners are definitely involved in it also (see Figure 2.2). Understanding the needs of the learners is vital. By thinking about what learners expect and what they need, by gathering as much information as is feasible, we can also bring the learner into the planning process even before they arrive. By building on such data, we lay a foundation for learning opportunities that accurately address the contexts and needs of the learners. This foundation will likely be adjusted, corrected, and refined, but it is a starting point based on the learners' experiences.

As stated previously, when considering these needs, we pay careful attention to the context, environment, organizational climate, supervisory expectations, learner responsibilities, and outside pressures. Needs assessment that serves as a basis for building transformative learning opportunities needs to delve deeper than cognitive descriptors and expectations of the learners. Learners continually approach their learning from different perspectives, roles, and purposes. We know that when we "connect" with adult learners' lived needs something powerful happens and we see motivation, understanding, and application move forward together. We must understand our learners and realize that transformative learning opportunities include critical reflection on their experience and understanding. We then incorporate learners' needs and contexts in preplanning, thus opening a vast and valuable storehouse of resources.

Another set of critical considerations in planning these learning opportunities is in the area of possibilities and reality. As we approach the entirety of the learning experience we need to know what learners need and what might be possible. Foremost in our planning we need to consult with the prospective learners, and then dream "large" – dream of the possibilities, the resources that would be available in a perfect world, and the dynamics that are powerful components of learning experiences. Without spending a copious amount of time in this step, such brainstorming opens up the creative energies so that we can think beyond the boundaries we usually have in place for our teaching and learning experience. Building upon those grand ideas, we must still face reality and prioritize and sort out ideas based on what resources we have, those we might be able to obtain, and those that are currently beyond our reach.

Now comes the time to match up resources with needs, and devise a plan to unfold transformative learning opportunities. If we conduct preplanning without reviewing resources, we may spin our wheels as our valuable ideas and plans will not have the support needed. Sometimes it takes resourcefulness to be able to gain access to the resources that will make a learning plan successful. Yet, if after careful consideration it may be worth the investment time and other resources to pursue obtaining what is needed. Possibilities for additional resources such as equipment, instructional materials, or personnel can include securing them through borrowing, sharing, renting, purchasing, or pursuing donations or grants. Where resources will be used over and again in several different ways, the value of securing them increases. In this way, we need to balance the acquiring of resources with an informal cost-benefit analysis of money, time, and benefits. However, this step in preplanning research can produce valuable new possibilities and opportunities for the learners.

Additionally, preplanning needs to take into account the environment where teaching and learning will be taking place. As we consider how we want to build learning experiences we have to be mindful of the setting both in preparation and with the learners' assistance as described earlier in the discussion of Layer 1. If unfamiliar with the site, certainly we would visit or at least gain accurate information about it. Transformative learning opportunities by nature include dialogue along with critical reflection, so there must be the capability for learners to be able to congregate for discussion. Tables and chairs bolted to the ground or an auditorium setting are special challenges that need to be addressed from the start. We have to consider how to facilitate conversation within the specific environment in which we will be working with the learners.

Finally, with transformative learning we also must reconsider issues of safety and trust in the learning settings; these are issues of great consequence. If there are relatively easy ways to build an inviting climate, then we should certainly pursue them. The value of creating a welcoming, warm environment needs to be interpreted for each group of learners and participating in the planning of their learning experiences can be powerful. This inviting environment needs to include affective, practical, and physical dimensions. Building a climate of safety and trust entails discussing guidelines of respect and confidentiality. Cultivating experiences of disclosure and acceptance creates an environment where adults can question and grow. Additionally, the affective and physical environment can be closely related and we need to work with learners to build this climate as well. Examples to this end can include having program breaks, debriefing, planning, sharing and activity times, bringing in light refreshments, providing hot or cold drinks, having comfortable furniture, or providing an assortment of background music. It is very important that we determine what makes our learners comfortable and at ease, not just what works for ourselves as the elements might be quite different. Now the stage is set to enter the practice stage of the model.

Practice

As we meet with the learners, we can use this array of possibilities together with information and direction provided by the group so that either they or we plot a preliminary plan for action. As learners engage with us in pursuing learning they become active agents in seeing how the model can help unfold the experience. This team is variously involved in building safety and trust, discussing needs, engaging in learning experiences, revisiting and evaluating, and revising and informing transformative learning opportunities.

Certainly there are many lines of action in progress as the learning unfolds and we can be best prepared for this by thinking through each strand of the model beforehand. Being able to discern where the experience currently is and where it needs to go, whether learners need our direct intervention or more hands-off facilitation become important aspects for us to monitor throughout the process.

The Transformative Learning Opportunities Model supports building learning experiences with branching possibilities that remain open-ended. Again, this process is not lockstep; it is an open, dynamic progression that can be adapted to evolving needs and interpreted within the context. The model can be interpreted and used by educators of different teaching styles and with learners who have a variety of learning styles, because it is not strictly delineated in one form. The following recommendations are helpful.

Building upon the preplanning research stage, practice is commenced with a continued focus on climate, safety, and trust. Those elements that have been considered prior to the meeting time are now put into action as the learners make contributions and adjustments to the environment so that their comfort and ease are maximized. We might also ask our learners to review guidelines for participant behavior, response, and confidentiality so that revisions can be made to fit the group and in so doing address their needs and build a foundation for trust.

As educators we have several ways to plan to discuss needs of learners and we have mentioned that it depends on the amount of time available. A good strategy is to prepare a list of likely needs and objectives that can be used as starting points if need be. Facilitation of this discussion needs to be rather open-ended so that based on what the learners determine, we are ready to suggest or co-create objectives and learning experiences.

In deciding what instructional strategies to use, we can bring together several options to develop the kind of learning experiences we intend to create. The learners' experience of the Transformative Learning Opportunities Model (Layer 1) reveals that educators should pay close attention to critical reflection, dialogue, and application. These are foundational elements for creating learning opportunities that may become transformative learning experiences. Using a broad spectrum of choices to build a collective design and including other instructional strategies can create powerful combinations. The resource list of instructional strategies found in Appendix G will be helpful here.

In the practice stage, we must remember to loosely compose a group of experiences that include the essential elements and yet meet needs through branching in different directions. These learning experiences are pursued with an open agenda to use what will best meet the learners' needs. Certainly this is not a highly prescriptive process and can instead be a beneficial opportunity for educator and learners alike to collaboratively develop the objectives and create the learning encounter.

In evaluation terminology we also need to be involved in forma-tive evaluation; in this context perhaps the phrase "formative develop-ment" would be more appropriate. King (2003/2001) describes an instructional design process for integrating new technologies into teach-ing and learning. This design includes ongoing evaluation of progress, determination of success of strategies, and the formative development of new initiatives all within the same learning experiences. Like that pro-cess, rather than waiting until the end of a learning experience, educa-tors take hold of the opportunities *throughout* the learning experience to clarify instructions, amplify needs, and pursue new directions.

Another key component of this guideline is that evaluation is not only focused on learners, but also on educators and the learning process. The traditional focus of evaluating learners or learning is of course im-portant (Dean, 2002); this focus is understood as the piece stakeholders value the most. However we must also, as reflective practitioners, evalu-ate ourselves as educators, consider how our work progressed, and de-termine what needs to be changed (Apps, 1991; Brookfield, 1990, 1995; Cranton, 1994, 2001; King, 2002). It is from this vantage point that we can reframe our role, bring in what is needed, and see different results if we put into action what has been happening within these transforma-tive learning opportunities.

Finally, we also need to critically evaluate our instructional plan (Dean, 2002; Lawler & King, 2000) and consider what works and what doesn't. We need to look back over the hour, the session, and the curricu-lum and ask, How can it be done better? What did we learn was needed? How can we best address those needs and concerns next time? One of the most powerful tools we have as educators is our experience that has been critically evaluated and revised. Building on this growing history with transformative learning experiences builds a reservoir of possibilities to draw upon in the next learning opportunity.

Educators preparing to create transformative learning opportu-nities can look at this stage of practice as praxis. It will never be perfect, it always has more possibilities, and we construct it uniquely each time. Not confined to a scientific deterministic model, the considerations in-cluded in the Transformative Learning Opportunities Model encourage, inspire, and provide a vision of what is possible as we engage in thought-fully developing and facilitating transformative learning opportunities based on the context and needs of adult learners.

THE TRANFORMATIVE LEARNING OPPORTUNITIES MODEL

The detailed view of the model (Figure 2.4) reveals the critical interdependent relationships of the planning and activities. Specifically, this figure uses overlays, like transparencies, to emphasize that the work of the educator proceeds from, and continues concurrently with, the experience of the learners. The overlays enable us to visualize and think about the coexistence and interdependence of these two pathways.

As planning, practice, and evaluation continue throughout the process, educators and learners move back and forth among the guidelines and stages. This structure is meant to loosely guide our conceptualization and teaching and learning activities. And yet, at the same time, the fully delineated model offers a framework that is consistent with transformative learning, particularly in identifying learner needs, building safety and trust, cultivating critical reflection and dialogue, and envisioning application.

Following the model leads to countless development, evolution, and branching possibilities. Chapter 3 gives specific details of how the model may be applied to a variety of contexts of adult learning.

SUMMARY

In this chapter the why, what, and how of the Transformative Learning Opportunities Model have been presented. This chapter began with a discussion of the benefits and limitations of this model. The model was then presented in detail both conceptually and through illustrations. As the model was explained, hopefully a vision of the possibilities for creating transformative learning opportunities became vivid for the reader. This discussion was meant to stir ideas about what the model could mean for your adult learners in your specific settings.

The final portion of the chapter brought us back again to application as we considered how we can prepare to use the model. Recognizing that we need to start with self-assessment brings us to evaluating where we are in our practice of adult education and to actively participate in reflective practice before and during our teaching experiences. The preplanning research stage was next considered in starting from the real needs of the learner and creating several options for learning that address those needs, build a safe environment, and address multiple pur-

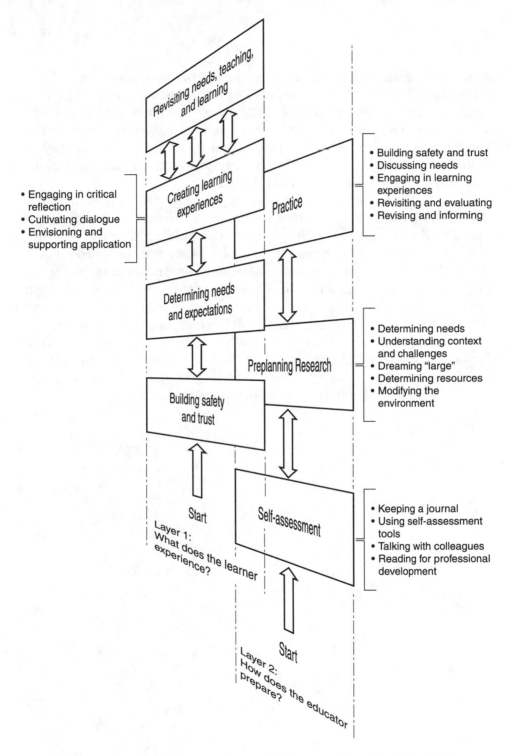

Figure 2.4 The Transformative Learning Opportunities Model in detail.

poses or directions. As the model enters the practice stage, the educator has possibilities laid forth and meets with the learners to chart an initial course, monitor the ongoing needs and developments, and guide learners in being involved in as little or much of transformative learning as they desire. This process is characterized by formative and flexible development and is a powerful framework to guide learning experiences into transformative learning opportunities.

The Transformative Learning Opportunities Model provides a flexible, open-ended, yet formatted direction for creating learning experiences that can lead to transformation. The guiding frame of the model reveals how it may be experienced and how we can prepare for it. By itself, the model, as an instructional design construction, is lifeless. It is only when adult educators and learners capture its dynamic and guiding framework that the power of transformative learning can come forth. When we adopt or interpret the model, we bring it to the unique and potentially powerful destinations of our choosing and making. The Transformative Learning Opportunities Model is a framework to guide the building of learning opportunities that may transform. For easy reference, Figures 2.1 through 2.4 are also found in Appendix A.

CHAPTER 3

The Transformative Learning Opportunities Model in Action

As we look at the Transformative Learning Opportunities Model, we see a framework that can guide our understanding, practice, and vision of teaching and learning among adult learners (Appendix A). Designing activities and engaging learners in discovering more about themselves and their understandings about content areas and through their experience becomes a guide for our work. Active learning, critical thinking, and reflective practice are key elements in this framework. In addition, a learner-centered approach that includes learners in planning, delivery, and evaluation introduces or develops a new dimension in our teaching and learning understanding and practice.

This chapter explores how the Transformative Learning Opportunities Model can be put into action in five general settings: continuing higher education, ESOL, ABE, workplace, and faculty development. The model is about best practice in adult learning, but also has at its core the dramatic transformation of adult learners. The common approach in this chapter is an introductory scenario and description to capture the setting. Characterization of adult learners and their needs in these contexts are also developed. Next, the view of developing transformative learning opportunities is placed within each setting to see how contextualization might progress. For each context, a specific learning activity is presented and explained with additional detailed materials available in the appendixes. Finally, examples of teaching strategies that might be used with these specific activities and more generally in these contexts are presented and discussed. It is expected that you may not read all the scenarios in this chapter in depth, but may focus on those closely relevant to the settings in which you work.

The matching appendix for each section has additional material to guide the use of the Transformative Learning Opportunities Model. A major point of the model is for us as reflective educators to engage in self-assessment, do the preplanning research, and then facilitate learn-

ing experiences. For this reason, the appendix for each context will begin with a preliminary series of questions and activities with which we
can engage. Next, the materials move into illustrations, suggested learning activities, and questions to guide the development of teaching and
learning experiences. Our focus is on the learning setting.

CONTINUING HIGHER EDUCATION

Continuing higher education particularly addresses learners returning to higher education after time away from the classroom. Rather
than the traditional undergraduate student who has recently graduated
from high school, these learners are adults who have begun or continued
their academic studies later in life. Continuing higher education is a
broad area that includes undergraduate studies across content areas and
disciplines, such as liberal arts and sciences, and professional schools
such as graduate business, education, social work, nursing, and medicine.

Whether we are language teachers, biologists, accountants, phar-
macists, or historians, we are specialists in our content areas, but we
may not have had preparation in teaching and learning. In this setting
the concept of developing transformative learning opportunities has specific challenges and opportunities. First, continuing higher education
faculty may not be familiar with the concept and, second, learners may
have specific career- and goal-directed purposes for their studies. However, transformative learning holds great promise for cultivating critical
thinking and introducing learners to new paradigms of understanding.

Sociology 101: Diversity

*The students arrive at the classroom dressed in business attire
and laden with lunch bags and cups of coffee. Obviously this is not a
"typical" freshman Sociology 101 class. Instead it is early evening and
these students arrive after having already put in a full day of work.*

*The students are from across various programs including busi-
ness, nursing, chemistry, social services, and education. They come together because they need an entry-level social sciences requirement; they
may or may not be particularly interested in this specific subject. However the motivation is high because they are students by choice and have
overcome obstacles continually as they persevere on this difficult road of
pursuing formal education during their adult years.*

As the students assemble, they do not isolate themselves, but in-stead gather in small groups and immediately start opening notebooks and discussing matters enthusiastically. At 7:00 p.m. the professor, Mar-tin, enters and the students barely notice as they continue, deeply invested in their work. When 7:15 pm arrives, Martin calls the class together with discussion questions displayed on the board and in response the students move their chairs into a circle.

The students developed the discussion questions two weeks ago in response to case studies they had been given. Since then they have been working in small groups to research information on and arrive at re-sponses. Martin starts the discussion session with a series of open-ended questions about the group process and how people may have varied per-spectives based on their personal and cultural histories. Using an example from his own experience, he reveals how his cultural background has obscured his understanding of some ethnic groups in the past. He then refers to the discussion questions and asks the class how they used the first case, about a gay couple moving into a working-class family neigh-borhood, to help understand not only themselves, but also others. A sample of the questions that the class had developed include the following:

- *What would be my initial reaction to the situation?*
- *Why would I react that way?*
- *What would be my unspoken and spoken comments to my neighbors and to the couple?*
- *Would I have fears or hesitation?*
- *Where could such feelings come from (culture, family, friends, etc.)?*
- *Why have I, or should I have, accepted them as valid?*
- *In what sense am I part of different subgroups in our society (religion, race, class, family history, etc.)?*
- *How do I feel when I am treated differently or unjustly?*
- *How could I step beyond my preconceived expectations and stereo-types?*
- *How have I responded to people different from myself in my neighbor-hood or at work?*
- *What conflicts or difficulties have I seen or would I expect?*

The class then begins to share some of their specific, personal ex-amples and excerpts from the discussion that the groups had about the questions. This initial discussion in the class decidedly focuses on the learners. Martin sits in the circle, and the students speak to everyone in the class and explore the meaning of responses with questions to one another. This discussion is central to the course topic for the past two weeks, "Understanding diverse people groups and personal, cultural history", but the class moves along in a manner quite separate from the pages of the textbooks. Instead of remaining in theory apart from their experiences, the students engage in discussing the issues of their lives. They press forward trying to understand how other cultural groups see their lives and perspectives so differently and to examine their personal and cultural responses to people different from themselves. Building such learning experiences in the classroom provides a vivid microcosm of the diversity of their larger world.

One of the major tasks of the professor is to facilitate the discussion, sharing in an environment that is appreciative and validating for different experiences and perspectives. The content flows from life experiences and the "curriculum" evolves, case study after case study, as students critically examine their own perspectives and seek to understand one another. In an environment where they have come to know one another, they know they can share their thoughts, even ones not entirely socially acceptable, and they will not be browbeaten. The discussion is more than academic consideration of questions and answers. Instead, it is a dialogue within which learners invest and seek to understand themselves and one another better. They contemplate, consider, deliberate, and even wrestle with substantial questions that do not have simple answers. They engage together to build new understandings.

The learners have selected groups to work in and focus their discussions on the case studies. The groups have three guidelines:

1. Have respect for other opinions.
2. Allow equal time for members to speak.
3. Collectively question reasons for views and decisions.

Within this model the groups discuss the cases each week and focus on the questions they have developed. The goal of the group time is to hear and probe each other's opinions and ideas and to collectively develop a plan for action in each situation. After this is done, each student writes a short email journal entry to the professor that states a personal perspective on the group decision.

During group time, the professor circulates to answer questions and address any difficulties that arise. Martin wants this experience to focus on students understanding not only the issues, but also the process of clarifying their values and beliefs through dialogue with their peers. Within this context, disagreements and emotional eruptions can occur and the groups may ask for his intervention to solve disputes. However, Martin will not "solve" problems, but reflect the circumstances and issues to the group for them to negotiate solutions.

Learner Educational Needs

These adult learners often pursue their studies amid the multiple demands of work and family. Pulled in many directions for their attention and time, they choose to invest time and effort in pursuing further academic studies. For many of them the purpose of their continued education is for career advancement or other change. Yet, even though it is related to their full-time responsibilities, the load of courses and studies is piled on top of already overtaxed schedules. Because of the challenges they face, adult learners tend to be highly motivated. They are often taking on these classes as additional activities because they want to move ahead or make changes in their lives. Continuing higher education learners are also an increasingly diverse population. Coming from a wide range of prior experiences, family and cultural values, and educational and career aspirations, their multiple needs and perspectives are more evident than ever. All of these factors contribute to high goals and great determination as these adult learners pursue their formal education. They are invested in their learning in more ways than one and they are committed to getting the most from their education that they can.

Transformative Learning Opportunities

How does transformative learning fit into career-focused study? As adult learners return to school they often have specific career or personal goals in mind. Within this context we can also view them as adult learners engaged in new pursuits to expand their understanding and open doors of new possibilities for themselves (King, 1998). The explicit goals are complemented by the need for adults to constantly cope with new responsibilities, demands, needs, views, and the future. Transformative learning opportunities can provide experiences of assessing new data and perspectives, trying to make these fit into current understandings, engaging in questioning prior beliefs, values, or assumptions with peers, and developing new understandings. Transformative learning affords an understanding of how to manage and learn from experiences. Education that is pursued with such learning in mind can take advantage of the ability of adults to develop new ways of coping with and processing new information (Mezirow, 1997). Transformative learning can be a perspective of continuing, lifelong learning for adult learners to build on their specific career goals and reach far into the future.

When continuing higher education learners engage in critically questioning new learning, examining the deeper meaning and questions behind public opinion and accepted knowledge, when they turn a critical eye towards themselves and examine their assumptions and beliefs, such as in potential responses in the case of the gay couple, they are developing dynamic means of learning for a lifetime. Whether they are in a sociology or nursing class, business math or basic English, learners develop the means to examine situations and information for deeper meaning, to bring them alongside of their current understanding, and to examine implications and consequences. They may also "try out" new views, test the "fit," and finally decide if and how such significant changes have a new place in their lives. A larger decision may be whether their greater frame of reference or way of understanding needs revision. These are substantial changes. When learners engage in such activities, they discover and practice a powerful means of coping with the constant deluge of responsibilities, decisions, and changes they confront in their daily personal and professional lives.

They also now have at least a prototype experience of accepting new ideas as possibilities and of taking the view of the "Other." That means to step outside of their own provincialism and consider challenging questions about the origins and truth of their views and perspectives. Even more so they enter the possibilities of new ways of understanding as they talk with their peers about these matters. Transformative learning in its fullest form is about fundamental changes in the way adult learners understand the world. It is a dramatic shift in their frame of reference and impacts all areas of their understanding. As learners engage in critical questioning, seek understanding, try new perspectives, and deliberate multiple views and meanings individually and with others, they may start to create new constructions of understanding for themselves. Within or beyond the classroom they may more fully enter into the transformative learning experience and eventually reintegrate new frames of understanding into their lives.

Continuing higher education learners often embark on or continue in professional careers that entail decision making moment by moment. In the workplace, employers and supervisors highly value the ability to critically examine information and situations and construct solutions. Transformative learning opportunities can provide experience and practice of these skills with real-life settings and substantial questions. The classroom becomes an extension of their real worlds. Textbook learning does not need to be separated from application.

Teaching Strategies

Many instructional strategies, which include reflection and dialogue, are particularly well suited for facilitating transformative learning opportunities. This section presents several examples of such strategies, but is not meant to be an exhaustive discussion. Hopefully the information will inspire new ideas for facilitating transformative learning opportunities in continuing higher education classrooms.

Scenarios are brief, compelling renditions of real-life situations that can be used as the basis for thinking about what issues and dynamics need to be considered. In contrast, case studies present more detailed accounts in order to work through specifics of a situation. These expanded accounts provide a basis for discussion, problem posing, and solution building and can be effectively employed in small groups. The educator might also develop simulations in which the learners fulfill specific roles in a case and work through dialogue and solutions. Simulations can be most basically conducted through role playing in the classroom, but more fully experienced as learners have the opportunity to "step into" roles and work through a situation. For example, a group might develop a grant proposal to fund a research project or a business plan for a venture company. The key is that the learners take on the roles and actually proceed to work through the task that is incorporated in the simulation.

Other significant strategies can include students interacting with readings and class discussions in independent written form through journal writing or web-based discussion boards. They might journal in a free-form fashion or their reflections might be structured by guiding questions that the professor has provided or the class has developed. Using a web-based threaded discussion the learners could also respond to and post new reflective questions. Through the online forum they can then dialogue peer to peer and with the professor as they explore the meanings and implications of questions being considered. While journals provide space for extensive independent thinking, online threaded discussions move this process into an interpersonal space and allow learners' thoughts to be considered and further developed by others. Research has shown that in these situations learners spend a great deal of time composing their thoughts and responding to one another (King, 2001). The depth of dialogue and the level of interpersonal understanding far exceed that of the typical classroom because time is not a constraint in the same way. Whereas in the classroom professors and learners can often feel like they are playing "Beat the Clock," online discussions are available 24 hours a day, 7 days a week. Participants do not have to be assembled in the same space and at the same time to communicate, and they can take more time composing their responses.

Other strategies to consider include problem-based learning, debates, round-robin discussions, collaborative writing projects, and dramatic readings or short plays. A more complete list can be found in Appendix G. The emphasis of all of these strategies as used in this model is to provide opportunities for learners to examine content beliefs and assumptions in order to determine their meaning in new ways. The focus is critical inquiry that empowers adults in their ongoing self-directed learning across the lifespan. Being able to dialogue, reason, and analyze are fundamental skills for this purpose.

Appendix B includes a sample lesson and materials for continuing higher education classrooms, developing further the *Sociology 101: Diversity* example. The goal is to initiate our thinking about what other topics and activities might be effectively used to consider beliefs, values, and assumptions and explore new ways of thinking and new frameworks of understanding.

ADULT ENGLISH SPEAKERS OF OTHER LANGUAGES (ESOL)

Adult ESOL classes often provide a tremendous mix of learners with varying educational preparation, professions, nationalities, cultures, and languages. This condition offers many opportunities and challenges to design learning activities that can serve as a basis for possible transformative learning. In addition, adult ESOL learners are already prepared for significant challenge and change to occur through their learning experiences, because often they have taken great risks to pursue their formal education.

In this example, as the adult students assemble, their goals include English language learning. Their diverse prior learning experiences often result in multilevel classrooms even though adult education programs may group them by English language ability.

Reading American Literature:
Revealing New Perspectives and Questions

As the learners busily work analyzing the short story, Maggie, the teacher, watches from a corner of the room. Gradually she makes her way from group to group, settling down briefly to determine the direction and climate of the discussions. She also answers questions the learners have about the goals, activities, or process.

Earlier in the course, the learners selected three short stories from an annotated list of 15. They have selected one each for a historical piece, a contemporary author, and a racial perspective. After choosing the reading material, the group then discusses the issues they will address with each of them. The primary focus of the class is language learning. Written and oral progress both are the goals. At the same time, students can also use this opportunity to learn more about the American/host culture and are encouraged to develop questions that reach beyond the story's surface into the lives, beliefs, values, and cultures of the characters.

At this point, the learners have read the historical short story study. In their respective groups they discuss what the text and their research reveal about the specific time period. Some students see the historical setting very differently from others and the dialogue is about the similarities and differences of their observations.

This is the first such learning activity for this course and students approach Maggie several times to resolve differences of observations, interpretations, and opinions. Each time she redirects attention to their group to use their experience, understanding, and research rather than have her serve as an outside authority. One or two of the learners continue to struggle with the student-centered process, but Maggie encourages them to work together and rotates her presence, and limited input, among the groups. From past experience she knows that by the time they start the second short story most of the ESOL learners will have adjusted to this method, but right now they are still in a difficult transition stage.

She is encouraged with the research the learners are doing together about vocabulary, literary style, and historical and cultural contexts for their historical short story. Andre and Romona present their findings about the social and economic dimensions of American Colonial farm life conditions. Carlos interjects with similarities and differences within the same time period in his native Ecuador. Lynn compares the conditions to her

upbringing in rural Dominican Republic and notes that although condi-
tions similar to American Colonial times exist in her country today, farm
life conditions in the United States are now vastly different.

The group asks Lynn to repeat and define some of the terms she
used and then discusses the disparate conditions. Why are the countries
so different in their rural settings? Do the political or government struc-
tures make the difference? Is it solely a matter of economics? Or are there
more factors interacting to create the conditions? Lynn especially pursues
this line of thought and shares how the government does not assist farm-
ers in her country. She has never analyzed her government's actions be-
fore, but has some serious questions she shares with the group. They en-
courage her to continue her research and to consider what alternative
views might be consistent with her findings.

Lynn is encouraged by her group's comments to continue her de-
liberation of these serious issues. Although it is difficult for her to chal-
lenge her cultural understanding and traditions, her world is beginning
to look very different now. This approach of gathering information to test
policies and circumstances is a new orientation for her. Rather than ac-
cepting situations at face value, she thinks about questions of purpose,
motive, implications, and assumptions. She still has to cope with the so-
cial implications of this new orientation, but she is ready to take the risk.
She is looking at knowledge and learning differently as she becomes ac-
tive in creating her understanding rather than receiving it from others.
This orientation to learning is drastically different from the traditional
mode she has been accustomed to, but it opens many possibilities where
she can learn on her own and with her peers. Stepping forward as an
active, self-empowered learner is a drastic change from the model she has
been confined to. This can be a new world, her world. For Lynn the door-
way of transformative learning is opening before her and she has decided
to enter.

Learner and Educational Needs

These adults demonstrated many needs common among ESOL
learners. They certainly needed to learn the language, but more specifically they needed to learn written, oral, and aural English skills. While
learning vocabulary, sentence, and grammar constructions, they also compared the historical, cultural, and political backgrounds of the United
States to their native backgrounds. This approach builds upon the realization that learning the language in order to function effectively in a

host country goes much further than a language grammar book. Learners often need a learning environment that not only challenges them to pursue this difficult work, but also supports their efforts and welcomes their participation. Language learning necessitates the involvement of the learner in practicing reading, listening, and speaking. Without pursuing all of these facets actively, ESOL learners will not reach full proficiency and will be held back from fullest participation in the host culture.

Consistent with these needs, learners also seek transfer of learning as a focus of their ESOL experiences. Unless they can use what they learn in the classroom effectively in personal, social, and professional settings, the learning is separated and powerless in improving their survival and success.

It is common for ESOL learners to be in the midst of a "disorienting dilemma" when entering an ESOL classroom and hence positioned to experience transformative learning (King, 2000). Learners may be struggling with new living conditions, governmental requirements and agencies, strange and demanding school and medical systems, and the myriad requirements of coping with a strange host culture and language. In the midst of this upheaval, survival and success are unifying themes as ESOL learners need to find solutions to their needs and get to where they can experience success in their personal, social, and professional lives. Transformative learning offers possibilities of providing a new framework of understanding that can help them cope with the constant change inherent in their survival.

Transformative Learning Opportunities

By incorporating dialogue, simulations, and/or collaborative learning, ESOL learners can put their learning into action immediately. Transformative learning digs deeper into adults' understanding of themselves and their worlds. Such learning can be used to develop authentic experiences that access and articulate core beliefs and frames or reference and to reveal prior assumptions.

Within this context, these learners may find themselves questioning and analyzing their native culture and language, their preconceptions of the English language and U.S. culture, and their self-understanding (King, 2000; LaCava, 2002). How do they articulate these issues and conflicts with the host language? How can they use several avenues of expression (such as shared history, culture, rituals, or music) to create their understanding? How do they learn through others' questions? How can they help one another see different perspectives? How can they learn to question new ideas, information, and controversies as self-directed adult learners? They can learn to critically question, analyze information, seek out resources, and synthesize their views and understanding through classes that incorporate such experiences. Much more than isolated language skills in vocabulary and grammar, these ESOL learners have the opportunity to develop new ways of coping with change, experience lifelong learning, and create new understandings of their worlds. More than content alone, such learning strikes at the heart of changing frames of reference and ways of understanding that can be valuable in coping with the host culture over the years ahead.

Teaching Strategies

Many instructional strategies can facilitate transformative learning opportunities in the adult ESOL classroom. This example has focused on collaborative inquiry groups that help select study materials, objectives, and curriculum. By having the learners integrally participate in the planning, delivery, and learning processes, this strategy builds great depth of understanding of critical issues, and techniques for self-directed learning. Both elements are fundamental to experiencing transformative learning across the lifespan.

The teacher had initial objectives in mind for the students, but included them in deciding on the final lesson focus and designs. She worked to move away from a teacher-centered model to the role of a facilitator and a learner-centered classroom. Often teachers have to provide guidance in formulating initial questions and suggesting how a group can solve group dynamic or task execution problems. However, the focus is not only on content learning, but also on lifelong learning skills and perspectives.

The collaborative inquiry groups guided ESOL learners to grapple with advanced vocabulary, historical and cultural knowledge, research strategies, critical questioning of themselves and others, and English language communication through the three major venues of reading, listening, and speaking. Other instructional strategies that may be useful for these purposes include collaborative writing, problem-based learning, simulations, role-playing, case studies, and group presentations. Additional strategies are listed in Appendix G.

By emphasizing research, dialogue, and collaboration, ESOL

learners can engage in language learning for immediate purposes and in authentic communication contexts. The abilities they develop in communication through the host language are further extended into higher order thinking skills. These skills can provide a foundation for exploring and analyzing new ideas and developing new frames of reference for meaning making. Through transformative learning opportunities adult ESOL learners can begin to realize life-changing perspective transformations.

Appendix C includes materials to assist in further developing this transformative learning opportunity for adult ESOL learners. The teacher's work of self-assessment and preparation research is presented in the first section. Next comes the preliminary lesson outline. As described earlier, the intent is that these lesson outlines will be a starting point. Teachers and adult learners can consider their specific goals, objectives, and needs and develop their own specific and uniquely relevant plans for learning experiences that may open the doorway to transformative learning for some participants. The lesson described in Appendix C and in the ESOL example is *Reading American Literature: Revealing New Perspectives and Questions.*

ADULT BASIC EDUCATION (ABE)

Adult basic education learners often approach the classroom with hesitancy and fear. The fact that they are enrolled in ABE classes means that they have not had a successful educational experience in the usual, or normative, chronological sequence, and timeframe. These learners already feel exposed and demonstrate risk-taking in their courageous efforts.

ABE learners enroll in classes in order to conquer basic skills in reading, writing, and math. In the United States if they can read they have likely taken the Test of Adult Basic Education (TABE) during a program's assessment and placement process. Many times TABE scores and General Educational Development (GED) attainment are the solely articulated goals of these learners. They focus on reaching those goals and oftentimes need to be helped to see the bigger picture of the results and implications of their studies.

Herein lies one of the major challenges for ABE instructors who seek to introduce learners to lifelong learning experiences like transformative learning opportunities. These activities have to be crafted carefully to accomplish both the learners' immediate goals and these broader opportunities. In part, this can be achieved as learners adopt a vision of self-directed, lifelong learning. Often as they catch a glimpse of the autonomy and power included in such achievements, they are quick to see how transformative learning opportunities can benefit them greatly.

Renovation Project: Integrated Basic Skills

It is 6:30 pm and the students are making their way to their class. They come dressed in varied styles from saris to sweatpants, and uniforms to blue jeans. Many of these adult learners work full-time or multiple part-time jobs. Others are on public assistance but have to take classes in the evenings because of childcare needs. The class is vitally important to them because they are seeking to master basic skills that will help them better function in their work and personal lives.

These learners funnel into the classroom and go to their bookcases to retrieve their materials. They then gather in groups around tables to work on the project in progress. They spread floor plans, materials lists, and catalogs across the tables. The students have been assigned to work as teams and renovate a small warehouse into living quarters. While they begin with a sound structure with heating, cooling, and plumbing systems, they have to design a floor plan, divide up the floor space, and order materials for walls, flooring, electrical, plumbing, heating, and cooling. It is a mammoth task, but as a whole the class faces it with determination and excitement.

The learners had started off with a class discussion of possible projects they could work on and chose this one because the neighborhood has a few unused warehouses and a community organization is considering renovating one as a contractor's speculation model. The work they do on this project can help give the organization some ideas of possible layouts, costs, and time commitments. This classroom activity is an opportunity to take a real-life problem and build real solutions. However this possible project first met with substantial resistance. How can they possibly tackle such a huge assignment? Where will they get help? How will they be able to understand the technical requirements? What about all the calculations they will need to do? The questions had rushed forth from the group with great emotion. It was clear that fear was the primary obstacle and Charles, the instructor, had talked with them about how they might break each obstacle down so they could solve it. Gradually emotions lifted to hope and daring. Several learners had made a convincing case to give the project a try to see if they could do something for the community.

As they commence work this week, the students' increasing motivation and ingenuity are remarkable. The work is difficult for them, and the task a long one. However the project and learning fly along. Caught up in creating solutions, students hardly notice the many ways they practice and develop their reading, writing, and math skills. The groups have been carefully assigned to include students with different reading and math skill levels.

Strategically, the students break the project down into distinct, but interrelated miniprojects so they can work their way through the project systematically. At the same time if some students are absent on a certain day, other tasks can be pursued. Rather than a linear process, the tasks are interrelated and can be approached with flexibility. Tonight the group is working on partitioning rooms, so they are dividing wall lengths into 16" segments to determine how many 2"x 6" support studs they need. Activities such as these are practical examples of how they can learn and use fractions and decimals. They frame out doors and windows, while keeping track of the linear footage of materials. Once the materials are determined for the framing, they look through catalogs and online for door and window dimensions, styles, and part numbers. Finally, they measure the square footage of the wall space to determine how much sheetrock they need. One person keeps track of 2"x 6" framing materials; another, wall covering (sheetrock, paint, compound, etc.); and another, doors and windows. They work their way through each room systemically as they create lists for each room and also compile a master list for the entire project.

The teams have decided to assign specific responsibilities to different group members but they continuously work collaboratively in reading difficult vocabulary, calculating figures, and making decisions. This project reveals how much more these adults know about renovating homes than they thought they knew. Drawing on their experiences doing minor repairs in their own homes, using skills from jobs they have had, talking with and interviewing family, friends, and professionals about the project, and pooling their research to make informed decisions, this group moves each member into new dimensions of empowerment.

Charles works consistently at drawing focus away from himself, redirecting questions to the group, and suggesting, but not handing over, resources that can be obtained. The students have several activities interwoven into the project: daily class work examples, brief daily status reports, weekly reflective journals, and the final team project portfolio and presentation. As the students work though the project in each class meeting, they share samples of the class work and their final decisions for their project. In this way the instructor is able to see if they are having trouble with calculations, or struggling with vocabulary or understanding. They also provide a one-paragraph status report/essay at the end of each class, and hand in their individual journals each Monday. At the conclusion, they will have a completed project and a half-hour class presentation with each student participating. These strategies afford much data by which to evaluate students' work and chart their progress. Charles has developed a point system that provides numerical values to each activity and to performance levels.

Once a week Charles has troubleshooting sessions with each group. In addition to observations and the written work, this provides an opportunity to see who is contributing and what problems may be surfacing, and to evaluate student progress. These weekly conferences/sessions also guide the learners to explore deeper issues in the project and turn their focus to their learning, progress, and development.

During these sessions Charles facilitates discussion on several substantial matters. The group discusses what they accomplished that week, the difficulties they encountered, and the communication among group members. In particular they seek to understand if they have different opinions, ideas, or strategies. They discuss why they might be different or similar and what can be gained from different perspectives. For instance, why some people think they should price everything out themselves and others think they could have a hardware store compile the list for them? They talk about retail versus wholesale pricing and what that means for individual consumers and companies. They may also consider expectations on room dimensions and building materials based on their cultures, experiences, and preferences. They also need periodically to critically evaluate the current and future needs for the building to make sure they address such needs sufficiently. A major emphasis is to consider the assumptions behind their opinions and preferences and explore how their different perspectives contribute to understanding more about themselves, their learning, and their project.

Charles also engages the learners in metacognition, that is, thinking about their thinking, considering what thinking and problem-solving skills they use. Do they all individually work through the tasks and related problems the same way? And how do they work through problems and challenges as a group? Changing perspectives are encountered when they think about what they are learning from the group renovation project, because they realize they are experiencing different ways of working and learning. Sometimes there are clashes of opinions and the group members have to focus on listening to views different from their own. These are opportunities to look at and respect different opinions. Through the project, the students also become adept at asking each other questions about why they have certain opinions and feel a certain way. These questions sometimes cut directly to the issues. Such conversations encourage students to think about issues and assumptions regarding personal and cultural expectations, economic and social oppression, and empowerment.

Learners are encouraged to determine how these discussions and resulting changes fit into their frame of reference and way of thinking: Do their learning, abilities, or point of view look different to them now? And if so in what ways? Do they feel more confident about their ability to pursue such a complex project? What does that mean for them as adults and as adult learners? How are they going to apply the specific knowledge and the broader learning they gained to their testing experience and their personal and professional lives? For several learners this project is a landmark experience. Along with the restoration project being accomplished, they are restructuring their identities as self-directed learners. They can grasp hold of a mountainous intellectual task and create the solution. They can decipher basic technical instructions and master calculations. They are capable. This identity is drastically different from the one with which they started. They are becoming proactive, accomplished learners finding resources and building solutions.

Learner and Educational Needs

ABE learners have a great need to master specific skills. They also need to grow in confidence and self-efficacy (King & Wright, 2003). Project-based learning can be used to meet many of these needs. In this particular project the instructor turned the focus of learning to the students, and away from him. The learners stepped in proactively, while the instructor served as a facilitator. This strategy provided experience with and built patterns of self-directed and collaborative learning at the same time. ABE students who can be encouraged to draw on their experience, stretch their understanding, reach for new resources, and solve problems themselves learn beyond the scope of the TABE or other standardized tests. Critically examining opinions and positions for assumptions and options provides an open and vibrant perspective for decision making. These are lessons of life, empowerment, and lifelong learning. A decidedly different perspective of themselves and their world may grow out of this experience.

Transformative Learning Opportunities

For many of these learners there is usually encouragement and excitement. For a few there are major turning points of realizing they can do such a meaningful and important project. They engage in problem solving and are valuable contributors in a team. Most of all, *they can do it*. Having had many negative learning experiences before, such positive achievements are critical building blocks for ABE learners (King & Wright, 2003). When instructors can find effective ways to integrate self-learning, critical thinking, and basic skills into transformative learning opportunities, a powerhouse of human potential can be released.

While programs and students need to meet the extrinsic and curricular goals of testing, agencies, or themselves, transformative learning opportunities give people the chance to reach further into themselves and forward into their futures. Adult learners who realize the transformation from powerless to powerful, from passive to proactive, and from failure to accomplishment experience a dramatic shift in their way of understanding and relating to their worlds.

The stories of adult learners who make these transitions are legion and celebrated around the world by adult education associations. Learners like these are the reasons that men and women invest their lives in teaching literacy and basic skills to adults. In order to invest our lives in a marginalized vocation, the intrinsic reward has to be great. We find it in the lives of our learners, for their dramatic stories bring transformative learning to life.

Teaching Strategies

This sample scenario demonstrated several instructional strategies that can lead to transformative learning opportunities for ABE learners. Once again the focus is on critical thinking and dialogue. In ABE settings we cannot assume learners know appropriate or effective ways to work in small groups. If these are new experiences, it is time well spent to offer instruction, modeling, and facilitation. Certainly the learning regarding self, others, and content can be dynamic and positive in small groups. It can also be destructive if things get out of control.

As learners work together they can solve a problem or case study that has multidimensional issues and requires negotiated solutions. Simulations and role-playing can provide a complex rendition of real-world situations and problems. All of these activities bring transfer of learning into the immediacy of the classroom. Activities can be developed in which learners engage in using their reading, writing, and math skills in concert with critical analysis and their communication and problem-solving skills.

Alternatively educators can develop learning activities and curriculum that are mixtures of strategies (see Appendix G for more examples). Often part of class time is spent working on collaborative activities and other time is devoted to more traditional methods. The emphasis is on practicing skills that students will encounter in daily life and testing situations.

Appendix D further details the *Renovation Project: Integrated Basic Skills* lesson. It begins with a discussion of how ABE educators specifically can engage in self-assessment and preplanning research and then branches off into the specific lesson. These materials provide a guide to stir educators' thinking, a place to continue to build on valuable experience and expertise and to facilitate transformative learning opportunities. Very importantly they are not confining "cookbook" solutions to fit every situation, but instead are dynamic possibilities to be revised and reinterpreted liberally. Educators and learners bring transformative learning to life.

As educators prepare the preliminary directions that learning experiences may follow, as learners step into the planning and unleash their abilities, and as the dialogue stirs and cultivates understanding and difficult questions, significant learning can be unleashed. As individual adult learners carefully reflect on their deeper understandings, perspectives, and assumptions, transformative learning can begin to become a reality. Not an easy road, such experiences can be deeply challenging and risky, but educators and learners who work through these experiences build strategies for coping with change and challenges for a lifetime.

WORKPLACE LEARNING

As we consider the workplace in the 21st century we are constantly reminded that we are lifelong learners. Whether it is new products, procedures, requirements, or technology, adults in the workplace need to learn at an increasingly rapid rate. To this end many organizations have trainers and human resources developers on their staff full-time, others outsource these services and bring in training specialists for individual initiatives. Whether in these formal settings or on an informal basis adults engage in individual and collaborative learning throughout their workweek.

Learning in the workplace often focuses on transfer of learning. Education is not pursued solely for the edification and development of the individual, but instead is cast within the context of the organization. ESOL classes in hospitals enable workers to communicate with the other staff and the patients more fluently, management training classes cultivate the talents of workers rising to leadership positions in organizations, and technology learning in the manufacturing plant enables workers to skillfully master computer-aided manufacturing techniques they need on the production line.

At times when national and local economies are booming, organizations can afford to invest resources in honing the skills of its workers to meet the escalating challenges of production and service. When economic patterns are on a downturn, organizations can tap the potential of its workers to find better ways to do their work, improve services and production, and cultivate ideas and plans for additional sources of revenue.

Nonetheless, in the midst of global conditions and organizational needs stands the adult worker. Inherent in the human condition is not only the need to provide for basic necessities, but also the drive to meet personal financial goals and find a sense of worth, satisfaction, and accomplishment. When organizations reward workers for their commitment and quality service and also cultivate the inner drive for self-actualization and excellence, they reach into the power of human potential. Such organizations often find their form in learning communities that see beyond the corporate balance sheet to the potential of the members of an organization. Employees then become a community of learners who excel in identifying learning needs, determining paths of learning, pursuing their goals, and enjoying the accomplishment and generative power of new ideas, abilities and possibilities (Senge, 1990). An organization that is invested in a vision of human growth and potential has at its core the potential to tap the power of transformative learning.

Sanking Financial: Technology Learning and Customer Service

As the loan officers at Sanking Financial plug in their laptop com-

puters, they also discuss the case study for the day. The day before their 1.5 hour class each week they receive a case study by email and then start to discuss it via a web-based discussion board. These cases are about people like themselves learning technology in the financial lending field. The cases relate to more than just procedural, technical development and instead included personal and organizational issues of adjusting to change, creating better work environments, and envisioning new solutions. Employees consider the bigger questions behind the software they are learning and the real-life difficult issues of personal, community, and organizational change and growth.

Sanking Financial is a loan and mortgage company that fields most of its applications from the Internet. No longer confined to walk-in services, the loan officers, processors, and underwriters now deal with applications from around the country. Several difficulties have arisen. With all their procedures being computer-based, the technical side of their work has escalated in recent years. They also are making a transition to dealing with communicating with customers on sometimes delicate issues across great distances. The personal side of their work is in some ways more important than ever, because they have to bridge geographical distances and be able to serve people's very personal financial needs and difficulties through distancing elements of remote geography, technology, and requisite paperwork. It is evident that those loan officers who are able to get in touch with the personal needs of customers, recognize whether they are anxious or not, effectively and courteously respond to their questions, and clearly state the financial alternatives available through Sanking's loan products, are the most productive.

For these reasons, whenever new technologies and programs are introduced in the company, the leadership makes sure that the trainers like Frank also include how to integrate these technologies into effective communication and service for its current and future customers. The age-old value of customer-service is recognized as crucial even in a highly technology-driven industry. In order to accomplish these purposes the company always requests learner-centered project-based or case study training sessions. However this poses a serious obstacle for some of the loan officers, as they want traditional, lecture-style training sessions. They do not want to have to work on application; they just want technical "skills." This situation has further dimensions as it is seen over and again that many of these learners feel uneasy about making mistakes in front of their peers. The challenges faced by Frank therefore include navigating teaching and learning expectations and building a climate of trust and respect.

The loan officers have their laptops started up and are checking the most recent postings to the web-based discussion of the case study. They consider how to handle bankruptcies that applicants have not disclosed in their applications. The new technology is software that runs comprehensive financial inquiries about person's credit and legal histories. This new technology is more user-friendly than prior software, but also provides a depth and comprehensiveness that raises serious questions and complications of how to deal with delicate, many times embarrassing, circumstances.

Frank enters the room and asks how the class is faring. They discuss difficulties the loan officers have faced that week with the learning experience and the results from their on-line discussions. Participants are given time to speak, and their concerns are recognized as valid concerns. The group discusses how to address some of the concerns immediately, and others are listed for later discussion.

Gradually the discussion moves into the new format of "What-if" and Frank poses several scenarios of difficulties they might encounter with applicants. Several complex scenarios are posed and rapid-fire responses are expected. The learners are getting used to this format now and provide many responses to each case. Then Frank quickly moves to the next scenario. After a series of these interactions, he suddenly stops and says, "Where are the problems?" and this is the cue for the loan officers to dig deeper into the situations of the customers and consider the difficult questions, issues, and concerns they might have. This discussion is preparatory for the extended case they will consider later, but at this early point in the session they already uncover complexities and issues that oftentimes lie beneath the surface unaddressed. These classes dig deeper, "stirring the pot," as some people say, and cultivate deeper thoughts about the issues, complications, and implications of their work for their clients, themselves, and their organization.

At this point, the class moves into a more technical discussion of the software's new features and the attendant change in workflow. As Frank demonstrates the features on the projected computer screen, the learners follow the tutorial on their computers. Throughout the presentation Frank queries the learners about how the features fit into their current system, what is new, and what is the same. Not passive participants, instead the learners actively engage in processing and critically evaluating the integration of this new software into their work protocols and routines.

Next, the loan officers are given a sample problem file that has been hypothetically downloaded from the application site. They are not only to work through the software to evaluate the application, propose a product, and profile of services, but also to look for deeper issues, see where there are problem areas, and determine how they will gather further information and address the concerns with the customers. Once they do this individually they work in small groups to pool their findings and consider issues of troubleshooting, legal requirements, confidentiality, customer service, remediation, and conflict resolution.

For some of these Sanking Financial loan officers, this is an entirely different learning experience. Instead of having information delivered to them, they actively develop the questions to pursue, the application to the workplace, and collaborative solutions. In addition to the change in focus and format, they hone their critical thinking skills that move them beyond filling out computerized forms and following standard operating procedures. They are asked and expected to develop deeper questions, look further, and identify additional needs and solutions. While their focus is certainly selling Sanking Financial products, they have become critical inquirers into the needs of their customers and seek to develop solutions for and with them to best meet their needs.

This perspective is quite different from a year ago when these training sessions began. Now in the classroom and in their daily work the loan officers no longer focus on the mechanics of their work, but instead look at the multiple dimensions of needs represented by each client. Frank and the loan officers have brief weekly discussions to develop a series of questions for the loan officers to use to help reveal problems in clients' applications.

- *What are this client's short-term and long-term needs?*
- *How can the loan officer work with the client to meet these needs?*
- *How do these needs fit into the client's geographical context?*
- *What else might need to be considered that the client might not be aware of?*
- *How can the loan officer gather additional information?*
- *What problems might be embedded in a given application?*
- *What consequences could any of these problems have for the client?*
- *Are there additional possibilities that might be relevant in this situation?*
- *How might the client be looking at situations in a different way based on that person's geographical and cultural context, occupation, socioeconomicstatus, or extenuating circumstances?*

There are many more levels to consider when viewing applications in this way. It is a big shift in thinking for loan officers who have been in a more lockstep, automated system for years.

Some loan officers struggle with the learning and the process. Going beyond the usual routine of their work upsets their comfortable and efficient habits. Routines provide security and confidence in a busy, and at times unpredictable, industry like theirs. On top of this they have to actively participate in the training sessions rather than just watch a presentation or read a manual. This is difficult for some of the loan officers and is a stretching experience that makes them aware of very different perspectives and skills. It also introduces a whole new way of looking at their work and their lives. Building opportunities where they work as teams helps develop confidence, provides extra ideas, and makes the learning activities go quickly. Like Frank, all the trainers working with Sanking Financial are available for feedback, but for the most part the small groups are self-sustaining and share their ideas with the entire group during the weekly discussions.

Realizing that this is a significant shift of focus and responsibility for the loan officers, Frank incorporates room for questioning individually and collectively, problem-posing, solution-building, and substantial room for dialogue. The learners also discuss some of the questions online weekly, both live (a private chat room) and on the web-board. For instance, Frank asks them to discuss their learning expectations, their perceptions of themselves as learners, how they relate to the different learning activities, and what additional needs are raised through the process. The loan officers also explore the concepts of lifelong and self-directed learning and Frank facilitates conversations about their perceptions, comfort, and application of these items to their personal and professional lives. The interplay between online discussions, interactive class presentations, and small groups affords a variety of opportunities to hear and consider multiple views of relevant issues that the learners have identified. Frank is able to wrap all of these many instructional activities together into the weekly 1.5 hour sessions that feel cohesive and provide enough closure for confidence. At the same time the sessions sustain open-ended questions that continue to be cultivated through the online discussions and lead into the next sessions. An additional important aspect is that goals and issues that arise and do not fit into the current training are archived and used in the development of future training sessions.

Learner and Educational Needs

Frequently, organizations are faced with competing considerations of production and profit versus personal and organizational meaning making. When these seemingly competing forces can be brought together to merged or parallel goals, then multiple forces can combine to power solutions. The goal of building experiences that facilitate lifelong and self-directed learning many times serves as a valuable bridge in these cases. In the scenario above, the need for learning technical aspects of a software package was incorporated into deeper discussions about critical thinking, customer service, human relations, diversity, and problem-solving. In addition, learners confronted their traditional concepts and experiences of teaching and learning. In these ways multiple dimensions of each of these issues were exposed for consideration, reflection, and discussion.

At this point in time, many workplace learners' educational history is still primarily teacher-centered and traditional. Embedded within corporate training that facilitates transformative learning opportunities then is also the need to help learners move beyond such views and to envision and experience learner-centered, problem-posing, critical inquiry, and collaborative learning that substantially supports lifelong learning experiences. These are large challenges and it must be recognized that they are valid educational objectives in addition to the formal "content area" of training curriculum. Providing opportunities for learners to move along a continuum of seeing themselves as lifelong learners is a powerful accomplishment for organizations seeking to cultivate vibrant learning communities that reach the fuller potential of their members.

Transformative Learning Opportunities

While maintaining a critical emphasis on transfer of learning and bringing training to bear on their work responsibilities, transformative learning opportunities also cultivate minds that critically examine situations and pose solutions. Such opportunities broaden the perspective of the individual to think beyond a personal frame of reference and consider radically different views, rather than being trapped in one mindset. Transformative learning can open minds and experiences to multiple perspectives and multiple layers or dimensions. It can unleash potential to radically change the way that people understand their work and, much more broadly, their world. Workplace training can afford a variety of experiences to cultivate such critical inquiry and transformative learning.

As organizations realize that training can be a source of new directions and possibilities for individuals' potential, the better they will be able to envision the benefits of transformative learning opportunities. By asking questions of meaning, significance, and complexity rather than routinely going through the motions, adults become active participants in problem-posing and problem-solving. Being closer to the front line of where work is implemented, learners, like these loan officers, are positioned to discover and invent solutions in ways that trainers and management may not — an obvious benefit to the organization.

Teaching Strategies

As in the scenario, workplace trainers can use many active learning methods to cultivate transformative learning opportunities. The emphasis on critical thinking, discussion, and problem-posing is crucial. To this end case studies, class discussions, and collaborative learning groups are excellent choices. Additionally simulations, project-based learning, and problem-based learning give learners personal involvement in situations that they can solve along with their coworkers. Several of these strategies are mentioned in Appendix G. Employees can also probe the multiple dimensions of situations and complications for application to their own work and learning.

In all of this the trainer can take a director's role in laying out an initial learning sequence and then letting the participants determine a specific pathway for learning. Providing an outline approach and several options can facilitate employees' planning their own learning and hopefully develop vision for and self-efficacy in planning learning on their own. Rather then looking at corporate and workplace training as mastering a specific form of technology or developing a specific product, facilitating learning experiences of this sort can develop proactive lifelong learners. Such vision and empowerment can offer vicissitude and power to organizations seeking to excel in their fields and markets.

Appendix E offers a detailed outline to support the workplace learning described in *Sanking Financial: Technology Learning and Customer Service*. The section begins with the introduction of instructor self-assessment and preplanning research and then branches into the specific lesson. These materials provide a suggested outline for trainers and learners. They are meant to operationalize the Transformative Learning Opportunities Model in a form that brings us closer to application, but does not confine invention. This model is dynamic, generative, and open-ended; these materials are offered as samples that should be revised to fit specific contexts and learner needs. Within this purpose then the materials are liberating in providing examples. Transformative learning is brought to life through the experiences of trainers and learners who catch a vision of its possibilities for their contexts and learning needs. From it come new perspectives and frames of references for life.

FACULTY DEVELOPMENT

Educators in K-12 schools and higher education institutions face unique challenges in their own adult learning endeavors. Being so focused on their classroom learners, oftentimes they may not think of their own professional development needs. Indeed faculty development often is pursued with only the classroom and student achievement in mind. This adult learning perspective brings the focus to the needs and potential of faculty members themselves.

Certainly preparation of educators varies widely. In the United States, K-12 educators in public school systems generally complete a course of study in teacher education and satisfy a certification process. They learn about student needs and development, instructional strategies, theories of learning, assessment, and content areas to name a few major focuses.

Higher education faculty are usually experts in their field of study, with a graduate or terminal degree in their content area. Most likely they have had little preparation in teaching and learning other than their own experience as learners throughout the formal educational system. For this reason, professional development in higher education today often focuses on teaching and learning strategies, student achievement, and technology integration (King & Lawler, 2003).

In spite of the diverse preparation of these groups of educators, a common theme is evident. Their educational preparation, be it formal degree study or professional development, often focuses on the students and seldom addresses the educators' needs and perspectives as learners.

Within this context professional development that facilitates transformative learning opportunities can reveal new possibilities for dramatic changes in understanding, perspectives, and meaning-making for educators at all levels (King, 2002, 2003b). This scenario illustrates some strategies to develop a vision of lifelong learning to cope with the many and rapid changes educators face:

- Bring the focus to the educator's learning needs.
- Develop critical thinking strategies.
- Cultivate reflection on issues of meaning and assumptions.
- Promote opportunities for dialogue about deeper issues of teaching and learning.
- Cultivate self-directed learning strategies.

Learner-Centered Classrooms:
Collaborative Curriculum Development

From down the hall Sondra, the professional developer, can hear the activity in the meeting room, and upon entering finds the professors already in their work groups. They have been redesigning their curriculum to maximize the impact of integrating technology. However this is only the project at hand; the major intent is to provide the professors with the firsthand experiences of a learner-centered classroom. Most of the professors received their education through traditional, formal educational studies and have little experience with student-centered learning. They identified this as an urgent, major gap in their understanding as they reviewed the accrediting assessments their programs are undergoing. How can they create such classrooms if they have not experienced them for themselves? How will they know the benefits and pitfalls beyond textbook theory, if they do not work through the experiences? In consultation with Sondra, this group of faculty from the Russian Studies program will redesign their curriculum in an authentic, real-world form of learner-centered learning.

The professors first met with the faculty development director to discuss their interests in learning about this instructional perspective and determine how that department could assist them in meeting their goals. From this meeting it was evident that these professors are in crisis. They feel unprepared in instructional options, unsure of the meaning of learner-centered education, uncertain of what changes it would mean for them, and greatly pressured to find solutions to their dilemma. Sondra has a many faceted background in learner-centered learning and has worked in K-12, higher education, and corporate training settings, finding relevant and authentic ways to bring learner-centered orientations to the specific contexts. She met with the professors to determine if her skills and approach would meet their needs. Her ability to understand learner needs and risks affords a natural fit for the situation at hand and Sondra and the professors have teamed up to cope with the challenge.

Sondra serves as a consultant to the professors to help them draw out their intentions and hesitations, articulate goals and objectives, and draft a preliminary plan of action for their learning. They decide on a project-based format and set as their project the integration of technology into the Russian Studies curriculum. In so doing the professors divide up areas and tasks to develop the details of the revision. They try to build on their strengths in the division of work. Some do fact-finding research about educational technology in their content area, others research the changing accreditation standards, others contact colleagues to determine what programs in other colleges are doing, and another group consults with colleagues on campus to determine resources and strategies already available and being used. As the professors gather each week to report on their progress, they focus on the "what" of their learning, the content, but they also discuss the reflective teaching and learning journals they are keeping. As they work through the process, they build confidence.

Sondra initially helps them to develop some reflective questions to challenge their thinking and they have been adding to that list throughout the project. What is a learner-centered classroom? What does it look and sound like? Who are our learners and what experience do they have in learner-centered classrooms? How do I feel about being the center of learning in this professional development project? What am I learning about myself as a learner? Do I have certain preferences of learning, or particular dislikes? What do I value about teaching and learning? What do I want my learners to gain from their courses of study? What is my purpose in teaching my content area? What benefits are there to this instructional technique and focus? What drawbacks and difficulties are we encountering? Do I want to adopt a learner-centered model for my classroom? If so, where does it fit in appropriately and how do I go about introducing and implementing it?

The professors respond to these questions in their journals and during their 2-hour sessions. Half of the session time is spent in large or small groups debriefing on the process and discussing the meaning of their learning. Going beyond learning new instructional strategies, these professors engage in pursuing the deeper meaning for adopting and integrating new teaching and learning strategies. They kindle a fire of inquiry to determine their prior beliefs, values, and assumptions about their learning. Together they turn these questions into explicit discussions of value and meaning. They endeavor to find ways to question their prior assumptions and determine the risks, merits, drawbacks, and implications of change. They work not only to develop the redesign of their curriculum in relation to technology, but also to integrate learner-centered orientations, activities, and perspectives in their curriculum. On a deeper level, they consider the risk and meaning of learner-centered education for themselves, their learners, their program, and their university. More than curriculum change this is a transformational experience for some of them in reevaluating themselves, their work, and their purposes. It is a difficult road to look at these areas of their work. They are so invested in their teaching that to question their purposes and approaches is to challenge their identity. Working as a group of familiar colleagues has made this easier in some respects as they are not alone and the others experience the same hesitancies and risks. Apart from the personal development, these experiences also provide opportunities to effect programmatic and perhaps eventually institutional change. Engaging in transformative learning opportunities is the path to critical self-reflection and a dynamic vision of teaching and learning. Some of them will follow that road and continue to see what the deeper meaning is for ways of understanding teaching, learning, and themselves.

Learner and Educational Needs

Faculty are pressed in many directions. Called upon to master classroom teaching and management, student assessment, content area expertise, organizational service, and contribution to their respective fields, faculty many times can lose focus on their own learning needs. Professional development can shift that focus back to the teacher as learner.

In their planning, faculty and the professional developer can benefit from discussing questions like the following. What professional learning needs do faculty have? How can the developer serve as a resource to cultivate self-directed lifelong learning perspectives and strategies? How can the developer serve as a facilitator as faculty determine additional individual and collective needs?

Transformative Learning Opportunities

When professional development includes transformative learning opportunities, the focus of the institution and faculty alike is raised from the business of day-to-day responsibilities to the greater purposes and implications of their work. For example, in the scenario, as professors probed the meaning and purposes of teaching and learning for themselves individually and as a group, they created many opportunities for deeper understanding. Such activities can foster discussion of underlying perspectives and frames of reference and bring issues to the surface. When faculty understand themselves, their learners, teaching, and learning in different ways, it opens new avenues for development.

In the scenario above, this shift in understanding was a fundamental one for teaching and learning. Moving from a traditional teacher-centered orientation to learner-centered one is a significant shift that faculty have been trying to accomplish for many years. Orientations are rooted in professors' understandings of themselves and ways of understanding knowledge and learning. To experience change here involves a fundamental reframing of the self in relation to our work. Bringing learners to the forefront as proactive participants and directors of their learning in some ways turns the classroom on its head and can be a major change, even a perceived threat, for us as faculty. Transformative learning opportunities open the doorway to consider such changes, to consider the risk, count the cost, and try new ventures. By building environments in which faculty can engage in critical self-reflection with confidence, safety and trust, these learning experiences can develop into significant changes in frames of understanding and meaning making (King, 2002, 2003a).

Teaching Strategies

In co-creating faculty learning experiences that can lead to transformative learning opportunities, professional developers can use a wide variety of instructional strategies. Involving faculty in the planning, design, delivery, and evaluation of such learning experiences is paramount for learning in this area. Providing firsthand experience in planning and using a variety of instructional strategies enhance both faculty learning and classroom application.

Small and large group discussions, project-based learning, and problem solving teams are effective means of integrating dialogue and collaborative learning into professional development activities. Given the nature of faculty work, professors are linked with their colleagues in purpose, but may not be linked in the usual schedule of teaching and preparation. Building experience and strategies for utilizing dialogue and collaboration instills lifelong learning strategies into daily routines, a major benefit for transfer of learning.

Simulations, case studies, online dialogue, collaborative writing, and reflective personal journals can also be used to cultivate individual reflection and group dialogue. By bringing problematic situations into the open and considering meaning, implications, and possibilities, new perspectives are cultivated. Discussing a situation in-depth with a colleague often yields new understanding. Finding words to articulate our thoughts in writing forces us to use additional thought processes as well. When multiple instructional strategies are used together, they can build and complement one another to produce greater impact for the life of the learner, in this case the faculty member. To this end Appendix G has a more complete list of instructional strategies to facilitate transformative learning opportunities.

Appendix F provides materials that can serve as sample teaching and learning plans for transformative learning opportunities within professional development of faculty. The first section poses the developer's self-assessment and preplanning research framework as indicated in the Transformative Learning Opportunities Model. The next section focuses on this specific sample plan: *Learner-Centered Classrooms: Collaborative Curriculum Development*. These materials provide a starting point; they should not be used in literal cookbook fashion. Instead, they are models to revise. Specific plans for individual faculty needs and contexts can be designed by developers and the faculty together. The Transformative Learning Opportunities Model provides the means for a dynamic learning experience that should result in faculty learners exploring their understanding, trying new perspectives, and constructing their own meaning.

SUMMARY

This chapter has provided an extensive picture of the Transformative Learning Opportunities Model in action. The model is discussed and applied in each of five contexts: continuing higher education, ESOL, ABE, workplace learning, and professional development of educators.

Each section includes a scenario of how the model might be seen in progress, a discussion of adult learners' needs and transformative learning, and an overview of suggested instructional strategies for each context. Additionally, detailed planning and instructional materials for each context are found in Appendixes B through F. These materials include educators' self-assessment and preplanning research framework and then preliminary learning activities for facilitating transformative learning opportunities among their learners.

The intent is to take what has been the highly theoretical construct of transformative learning and bring it into the experience of teachers and learners. By discussing how such learning can be facilitated through a variety of classroom learning opportunities, the theory is brought to life. Transformative learning is certainly a highly individualized experience. The accounts and explanations presented here are not meant to confine our definition or understanding. Instead it is hoped that these descriptions and perspectives will open our understanding further to consider the multitude of interpretations transformative learning may have in the lives of adult learners. In the venture of learning across their lifetimes, adults have the potential to continually master and transform the challenges of learning for their own development.

CHAPTER 4

For the Educator: The Vital Role of Reflection and Evaluation

Chiuang

As Chiuang heads to his car he mulls over his teaching of the professional development session on distance learning and human relations. He knows his thoughts on the ride home will center on debriefing the class and writing in his online journal later that night. Chiuang finds himself playing over key scenes from the session as he thinks about the faculty responses, their questions, and plans for action. He recognizes that his work with faculty extends beyond learning skills for online teaching and learning, to cultivating a climate of contemplation, discovery, and reflection and facilitating consideration of the human and personal issues involved.

As he steers toward the highway, Chiuang is thinking about Anna, an engineering professor, who listened intensely to the presentation and honed in on several issues during the discussion. Anna was very concerned that her learners be experienced and proficient in working in teams to accomplish technical projects. What is it that catches Chiuang's attention? Is it that the professor so values her learners' achievements or is it the seeming contrast between technical learning and social communication skills? Sometimes people think of technical fields as "cut and dried" learning that leaves little room for human differences and needs. This juxtaposition of technical and social communication skills intrigues him as it brings his thoughts to the question of how learners learn best. What about the engineering students and what about the faculty at the college? Are they keyed into needs learners have when working on team projects? Will they know how to facilitate such teams? Will most of them even value and create work group activities for their classes? And what about himself? When does he have faculty work on group projects? He values collaboration for many reasons, but why does he not use this more in his professional development sessions?

These thoughts bring him to considering project-based and col-

laborative learning and Chiuang realizes that if he values these types of learning, he should be modeling them in his classes. Why has he not done this before? Chiuang thinks it may be time constraints and the technical skills that faculty so urgently need to learn. Chiuang works through an instructional design outline in his mind. He begins to clarify his goals and objectives for working with faculty in general and for addressing specific needs in these faculty development sessions. How can he bring these disparate goals together into an effective format? What will he do differently next time?

Chiuang's stream of consciousness is not so unusual for the reflective practitioner. So often as we engage in facilitating classes and later leave the learning environment, we run through this sort of commentary and teaching and learning evaluation. Different personalities may focus on different issues during their reflection in part because some gravitate more toward the negative, others toward the positive, and some highlight process over outcomes. Whatever our propensities, engaging in reflection about teaching and learning experiences is invaluable in improving our understanding and performance, and our learner's benefits.

In this chapter, the focus is on the work of the educator within the framework of the Transformative Learning Opportunities Model (Appendix A). In particular, this chapter presents possibilities for reflective practice that educators of adults can use to assess their teaching and learning. Starting with ourselves as learners, this discussion unfolds the concept and reality that incorporating opportunities for reflection-in-action and reflection-on-action can provide us with a broader perspective. From this broader perspective the role of transformative learning will be considered and the focus for student learning shifts to include critically reflective thinking, growth, development, and the construction of knowledge within the content area.

Related to this broader perspective, it is evident that standard assessments do not always meet the need for transformative learning gains. Therefore alternative models of assessment and learning activities for both teachers and learners are presented. These examples include authentic assessment, portfolios, problem-based assessment, and journaling, among others. The focus is on us as educators of adults and on our roles in reflection and evaluation in a model that brings transformative learning opportunities to the classroom.

EDUCATOR AS LEARNER

The model has two strands of action: educators' experiences and learners' experiences. This shared focus brings consideration of the educator to the forefront. Within a model that facilitates critical reflection and reexamination of beliefs, values, and assumptions among learners, it is critical for educators to have this perspective for themselves as well. The Transformative Learning Opportunities Model recognizes educators as essential facilitators in building preliminary learning experiences, guiding planning and inquiry, stirring deeper thoughts, extending learning opportunities, and cultivating lifelong learning perspectives and experiences. Such an educator is one who ascertains learning needs, charts a course, and supports learners' constructing their personalized educational experiences. What characterizes such adult educators? And how do they learn this perspective and practice?

The answer is at once simple and complex: we as educators are adult learners ourselves. Like those that we work with, we need to understand ourselves, consider our goals and objectives, examine our values and assumptions, and allow ourselves to embrace a vision of new understandings. We begin with a review of basic characteristics of adult learners. Among other salient adult learner characteristics, educators respond positively to a learning climate of respect, desire to be active participants in their learning, have substantial experience to build on, desire to learn for application, benefit from collaborative inquiry, and can be empowered by learning in their personal and professional lives (Lawler & King, 2000).

As we engage in our work of teaching and learning, we are learners who can use our past experience to guide our future efforts through reflective practice. In so doing, we can individually and collectively process our experiences in light of new concepts and experiences. As we engage in reflection-on-action, we can critically reflect on the meaning of our work, our purposes, and our impact (Schön, 1987). We can think about ourselves as learners and the ways we learn best and worst. We can think about what it means to be a confused or overwhelmed learner. We can remember through these experiences what questions and concerns learners have. When we take the position of the adult learner in our classrooms, we can see our work through a distinctly different, and revealing, lens.

Such reflection is at the heart of significant change and leads to opportunities to experience perspective transformation for ourselves (Cranton, 1996; King, 2002, 2003a). In the following scenario, consider how such experiences transpired for one educator.

Evelyn

As Evelyn signs into the web-based discussion she reminds herself that she has to catch up on this week's lesson. She has signed up for this 6-week course on distance education and has struggled from the beginning to keep up with the reading and online discussions. The reading is interesting, insightful, and enthralling. And therein lie the greatest difficulties. She gets so absorbed in the reading that she spends a lot of time writing in her reflective journal. Then she logs onto the bulletin board and finds that her colleagues have been posting critical questions, issues, and disagreements that take the reading and application even further.

By the second week she finds herself mentally stomping her foot and saying, I do not want to do this anymore. I do not want to sign into class! This overwhelming negative attitude is unexpected, even alarming, for her. She loves technology innovation and she loves to learn. What has happened to her? One evening she suddenly looks at herself differently and realizes, This is what online learning might feel like for some of my learners! This might be why some people are so reluctant to do the online work and why they can be behind by the third week and never catch up, even though they participate every week.

The time seems to fly when she is in the flow of her online work, but this is the summer semester. Imagine if it were the fall or spring! She never would be able to devote this much time and concentration. She starts to think about her learners and classes differently. She questions her assignment and reading loads for her online courses. She seeks new assessment techniques to try to uncover some of the learners' reactions and to include the new dimensions of their progress, the new directions that she is starting to see in her own experience. Evelyn begins to realize that learning does not have to be comprehensive. It can be selective and, furthermore, constructed and collaboratively invented through different technological capabilities. Suddenly she sees teaching and learning through a new frame of understanding. This is the beginning of a very different way of understanding knowledge. Evelyn begins to develop and experience new approaches to conceptualizing, creating, and facilitating teaching and learning experiences.

How could Evelyn benefit from this experience? In our account she had started to benefit already! Evelyn had taken an experience that was perplexing and frustrating to her — not wanting to learn online — and examined it in light of her teaching and learning experiences. She placed herself in the situation of her students and processed the thoughts and emotions she was experiencing. Then she examined her assumptions that learning was always fun, easy, and comfortable. She took her contradiction of experience and pushed it further to understand her classroom and the learners' perspectives better. Going beyond this reflection on her practice, Evelyn pressed questions of knowledge and learning as well. Was knowledge discovered or created? Was it individually gained or could it be socially constructed? These thoughts turned her world of teaching and learning upside down. But she persisted perhaps because she could see some greater possibilities and she had support from her colleagues who were having similar experiences. The point is that Evelyn took on the role and perspective of the adult learner and walked through the beginning of a transformative learning experience for herself. She knew this experience from a different side of the fence now and it was a compelling lesson in a virtual community of learners.

In Chapter 2 the Transformative Learning Opportunities Model was worked through step by step and educators' self-assessment was addressed in detail. What is vital here is to realize that critical reflection and self-assessment are the starting points for our work as educators in this model. We do not start out with rigid goals and objectives; we do not leap forward to instructional plans. Instead we pause to look at ourselves and ask why we engage in teaching and learning day after day, what our assumptions might be, and where we want to head next. By clarifying where we are and where we desire to go, we practice reflection-in-action (Schön, 1987). Rather than waiting until after the fact, we start from this orientation and as we proceed we remain mindful of the progress, meaning, and impact of the teaching-learning process. Being able to consider such questions while we engage in teaching and learning is a dynamic and meaningful additional dimension of the educator's experience. Rather than a linear progression, reflection-in-action provides many opportunities for formative redirection and refinement. Assessing ourselves as learners and as teachers we can examine many aspects of these experiences and provide a thoughtfully informed base for our professional work and development.

Reflection-on-action is more similar to the process Chiuang experienced at the beginning of the chapter. After the fact, with the experience fresh in our minds, we see the progression of action, thought, and impact as we play back our mental videotapes. Delving deeper into these experiences, we can consider issues of development, meaning, implications, and complications. As educators we can ask how to build on these experiences and what to do similarly or differently the next time. We begin to consider new dimensions of teaching and learning and plan new strategies. We try to align the learning experience closer to ours and our learners' values, goals, and needs. Reflective practice enables a broader perspective of our work as educators.

A BROADER PERSPECTIVE

Returning to the first scenario, Chiuang's experience with faculty development, colleagues in computer and technical services might have been puzzled by his focus on learner needs and application. Traditionally, distance learning professional development has focused on technical skill acquisition and improvement. Chiuang instead looked at educators as whole persons and concentrated on their needs as learners, the context in which they worked, the objectives and goals they needed to meet, the details of application to their learning contexts, and deeper questions of meaning and implication.

In the second scenario, Evelyn's experience revealed new dimensions of understanding her learners and teaching and learning. Rather than a single focus on her positive, smooth, and successful learning experiences, she now had additional experiences and viewpoints from which to regard teaching and learning. While much of her academic career had been targeted toward achievement and performance resulting in a high grade point average and academic awards, this difficult venture into online learning had humbled her expectations and elevated them at the same time.

Based on her six-week foray into online learning, Evelyn no longer assumed success in academic study. She had a new perspective of the complications and scheduling issues that students faced as their multiple responsibilities and constraints competed with their educational aspirations. Evelyn also looked at outcomes of learning differently now. Rather than a test score or skills measures, she looked at qualitative differences, personal gains, ways of understanding, development, and invention.

Self-assessment serves a vital role in the Transformative Learning Opportunities Model. Instead of building expectations solely on textbook or external expectations and measures, our self-assessment makes us the starting point in our preparation and understanding of learning experiences. Coming to the schoolhouse for ourselves and taking the role of the learner, we engage in reflective practice. Such experiences can build our understanding of ourselves and by extension our students through a lens of adult learning that is consistent with transformative learning.

Critical reflection, in its many different forms and dimensions, is seen by many as the heart of transformative learning. It is when the learner is placed in a quandary, a dilemma, a difficult condition of confusion, or a conflict that reassessment becomes vital. Perched on the edge of difficulty and conflict, we as educators, like other adult learners, may be more ready to ask difficult questions of our beliefs, our assumptions, and ourselves. As we ask ourselves these questions in a learning environment that is safe, respectful, and supportive, we can deliberate among ideas and positions and take risks in trying new viewpoints. When these experiences come together fully, we may experience a radical change in our way of understanding and discover a very different focus and sometimes meaning. At the core of this learning process are critical questioning, probing of meaning, and relentless pursuit of additional questions. When we travel this learning journey ourselves, we are freshly reminded of its meaning, risk, and impact and have an authentic experience from which to build transformative learning opportunities. No amount of academic study will suffice. We need to bring our own lives into the stark light of critical reflection in order to understand and support the experience among others authentically and fully. Teachers as learners bring transformative learning to life.

ASSESSING TEACHING AND LEARNING

A premiere issue in assessment is identifying learners' and organizations' needs, objectives, and goals. Bringing these concerns forward explicitly in the development stages ensures making clear for which target we are aiming, at least initially! Many ageless questions for educational theorists, researchers, and practitioners arise concerning assessment of teaching and learning (Angelo & Cross, 1993; Banta, Lund, Black & Oblander, 1996; Cross & Angelo, 1988; Courts & McInerney, 1993; Palomba & Banta, 1999). How can we further align our self-assessment with our practice? How can we construct more probing questions regarding teaching and learning throughout each stage of the model? Given that we start with self-assessment, how do we continue assessment throughout these experiences?

At the core of assessment are values of educators, learners, and organizations (Miller, Imrie, & Cox, 1998). Educators clarify these values through self-assessment and group discussions and decisions on learning goals and objectives. Our values can reveal the basis for our assessment activities. How then are we able to determine if the goals and objectives have been met, or that a transformative learning process has been experienced in some form? A dual approach is needed as content learning and transformative learning both need to be reviewed. Within the Transformative Learning Opportunities Model, assessment can be defined as determining not only the achievement of content goals and objectives, but also the impact of transformative learning on ways of understanding, emotions, and relationships, decisions, and actions that extend far beyond the traditional scope of the classroom. Assessment poses distinct challenges for educators adopting a stance like the Transformative Learning Opportunities Model and merits in-depth discussion for development of our understanding and practice.

Assessment Applied to Transformative Learning

As we have considered reflective practice through self-assessment among educators, we are reminded that the learning goals and objectives among our learners often extend beyond test scores and skills measures. Indeed, transformative learning theory has been greatly developed in the last 20 years not only to focus on its original domain of cognitive development, but also to include affective, spiritual, and multiple dimensions (Baumgartner, 2001; Daloz, 2000; Dirkx, 1997; Mezirow & Associates, 2000). At the same time, the process of transformative learning often includes discreet and yet related experiences of cognitive questioning, invested deliberation, contradictions, new possibilities, experimentation, risk-taking, and resolution. All this can possibly be experienced with little emotion, but most often learners depict difficult feelings, emotions, and consequences throughout. Often, these are not easy learnings in adults' lives, nor are they quick. Instead, learners describe difficult questions and decisions that they experience over lengths of time that range from months to years (King, 2000, 2003a, 2003b. King, Bennett, Perrera & Matewa, 2003). The Transformative Learning Opportunities Model represents a series of steps along that journey. Most likely they are not endpoints in the journey, but lead to further experiences of transformative learning. We seek to identify authentic representations of learning experienced in the transformative learning journey. These are our goals for teaching and learning and we need to have some appropriate ways to determine whether they are experienced or not.

Such experiences and learner development withstanding, educators face a tall order when seeking to assess transformative learning. How do we document or measure the quantitative and qualitative changes learners have as they go through these experiences? Realizing that in many sectors of adult learning quantitative evaluations are requisite, we must build a complement of multiple assessments. Even when the Test of Adult Basic Education (TABE), Graduate Record Examination (GRE), or certification tests are required for documenting progress, educators do not have to stop with these assessments alone. Instead, while educators build transformative learning opportunities to address the goals and objectives of the learners, their organizations, and the related tests, they also can develop and use alternative forms of assessment.

Although funding or certification agencies might require minimum test scores, it does not mean that adult learning experiences have to be limited to those parameters and dimensions of learning (King & Wright, 2003). For example, although learners may need to score 10th grade level on the TABE, their writing and critical thinking skills both can be developed through journaling and collaborative writing projects. By writing more frequently through journaling and also engaging in evaluating the work of their peers, learners may internalize many critical principles of effective writing and analysis. Certainly adults might need assistance in learning how to understand test-specific questions if they lack experience with the testing format, but the content of their learning can be embedded within learning experiences that have personal and professional depth. Such experiences can cultivate critical questioning and develop new understandings of perspectives of themselves and others, and provide a basis for self-directed lifelong learning that will benefit them in their personal and professional lives.

Types of Assessment

It is useful to consider the different types of assessment as diagnostic, formative, summative, and continuous (Miller, Imrie, & Cox, 1998). Each type complements another and together they provide powerful tools for evaluating student learning.

Diagnostic Assessment

Diagnostic assessment offers the capability of determining what level of achievement a learner currently has in a specific area of understanding or skill. It can also be used to identify differentiation of abilities or skills. In addition to such placement assessments, diagnostic assessments can identify areas of difficulty, and help teacher and learner to focus on the specific assistance a student might need.

When working with adult learners in some contexts, learning disabilities appear more often than in other settings. However, learners can be found in all settings who have specific physical, cognitive, or other disabilities. Diagnostic assessments can be used for placement of learners or when performance problems arise. Educators can usually find assistance in their educational programs or through educational counseling and psychological services that can assist in administering and/or evaluating such tests.

Formative Assessment

Formative assessments can be effectively employed throughout the teaching and learning process. By not waiting until the end of a series of learning experiences to gather information, we can have the advantage of being able to see progress, responses, and needs along the way. This advantage is capitalized on when we are able to adapt the learning plan to meet the needs that are identified. Formative assessment can be the lifeblood of success. Steering clear of emerging obstacles, recovering from mishap, and finding more suitable or refined goals, formative assessment can guide learning experiences that were headed for distress to success. The operative in such assessment is usually the educator. If we have not caught sight of the benefits of investing time and effort in and then utilizing the results of formative assessment, we cannot enter into this avenue of assistance and success.

Forms of formative assessment include tests, observations, interviews, focus groups, or questionnaires to name a few. Questionnaires may include free response or scales to rate, for instance, teaching methods, teacher performance, existing or changing learning needs, pace of learning, content relevance, group dynamics, and the physical comfort of the learning environment. Open-ended surveys can provide space for learners to register their concerns, fears, and successes. Additionally, learners might participate in focus groups to discuss their learning experiences, gains, needs, and preferences. These groups could include critical reflection, processing, or debriefing about the experience to explicitly tie the reflective process to learning that may be more technical or content specific. Quantitative or performance tests may also be used to chart the progress of learners according to specified goals and objectives.

Gathering this information during the learning process affords time to remediate difficulties and maximize success. For example, in some situations learners may reach the objectives more swiftly than anticipated and be ready to pursue further study immediately. In other cases, learners might be having difficulty early on in the course and need assistance in order to stay on track. Thus, using formative assessment and recognizing achievement or difficulty early in the experience can provide opportunities to consider and successfully navigate obstacles and accelerators to learning. When used to pursue questions of cause, meaning, and impact of learning, quantitative tests also can be incorporated into transformative learning opportunities. Going beyond achievement, these assessments can help educators and learners to explore the multiple dimensions of the learning experience and their lives.

Summative Assessment

Summative assessments provide a retrospective view of learning experiences. Near the end of sessions of courses, learners are often asked to evaluate the learning experience. Additionally, their progress is assessed at this point. The after-the-fact vantage point offers a comprehensive view that might not be available prior to that time. For example, learners may be able to see new connections among learning activities and purposes. Indeed, sometimes it is easier for learners to see their progress when it is more dramatic as from the beginning to the end of a series of events, rather than incrementally along the way.

In most cases, educational initiatives employ summative assessment to document student progress. Forms of summative assessment are innumerable. To name a few that can be used effectively with the

Transformative Learning Opportunities Model, portfolio assessments, self-evaluation essays, performance-based assessments, and skills or achievement testing emerge as valuable indicators. Indeed when students use portfolios to demonstrate their achievement, it can be a capstone demonstration of their learning. Performance-based assessment might be used through simulations in which students are observed in real-world-like situations to demonstrate their abilities. Self-evaluation essays are effective vehicles for learners to revisit and articulate their progress. Writing often generates new insights for learners and helps them examine the changes they have experienced. Such essays can lead to reflective questions and thoughts regarding the impact of the learning for their lives.

Continuous Assessment

Continuous assessment may incorporate all of the above types of assessment, but focus on progress and comprehensive evaluation. In its familiar use, Miller, Imrie and Cox (1998) refer to continuous assessment and focus on frequent testing over units of study without a final assessment. I think of continuous assessment more broadly. For instance, while starting the learning journey with an assessment of skills and needs, students also would be evaluated during the learning experiences and then more comprehensively at the end. In this manner, continuous assessment could include two or more forms of assessment and the impact could be compounded to create a synergy of assessment and insight throughout and after the learning experiences.

Many forms of assessment can be used across the learning experience in a continuous format. However some are distinctly suited and specific to this type including a chronological portfolio, reflective journals, unit tests, frequent tutorial sessions, or focus groups that could serve much like quality circles (Cornesky, 1993) from the days of Total Quality Management. Exploring innovative ways to help learners and teachers to track progress and needs can provide an infinite variety of continuous assessment configurations.

All of these types of assessment can be used in many ways. The power of assessment may be most evident in the principle of triangulation. Rather than taking a single slice of the learning experience in one form of evaluation, instead educators and learners engage in using several types and forms to afford a more complete representation of the learning experience and learner gains. Again, consistent with the Transformative Learning Opportunities Model, such an approach provides educators and learners with multiple dimensions or layers of learning and more likely represents assessment of transformative learning experiences.

ALTERNATIVE MODELS OF ASSESSMENT AND LEARNING ACTIVITIES

As stated above, transformative learning might not be evident through traditional forms of assessment. Given that many educators do not have formal preparation in assessment, and might not have experience with other than traditional testing and observation forms, this section presents some prominent alternative assessments and learning activities that can demonstrate content and transformative learning. Each section describes the assessment or activity, illustrates it, discusses assessment in that context, and demonstrates the connection to transformative learning.

Authentic Assessment

Authentic assessment has a variety of meanings in different educational and training contexts. For purposes here it means assessment that aims to evaluate learner progress in a mode as close as possible to how that learning will be used (Thomas, 2000). In other words, authentic assessment seeks to evaluate how well the learner can apply the learning. Ranging from problem-based learning, to performance assessment, portfolios, prior learning assessments, and prototype development, authentic assessment is a valuable means of delving beneath the surface of knowledge recall and requires learners to evidence their learning in real-life applications. This possibility brings assessment of content learning to a different level than many more familiar or traditional approaches.

Going further, authentic assessment can also chronicle how learners experience changes in their understanding, skills, and practice through demonstrated application. For example, a business student might design a prototype international business that synthesizes knowledge in marketing, strategic planning, accounting, global trade issues, writing skills, problem solving, and multicultural communication skills. When this final project is used as a basis for learners to reflect on the process, these experiences can become explicit contributors to developing transformative learning opportunities.

Two of the major problems associated with authentic assessment include determining guidelines for evaluation and the extensive time commitment for that evaluation. For example, in schools where prior learning assessments (PLAs) are used to qualify life experience for college credit, faculty may need to be specially prepared, objectives reconsidered and reframed, learning activities clearly defined, and considerable faculty time allocated for assessment (Thomas, 2000).

Authentic assessments are particularly relevant to the Transformative Learning Opportunities Model because they can also show how learners experienced change rather than being solely a quantitative measure of achievement. When combined with critical questioning, reflection, and dialogue, the product or data of authentic assessment can serve as complementary building blocks for the Transformative Learning Opportunities Model experience. Authentic assessments bring qualitative dimensions to the learning experience in order to illustrate multiple layers of meaning and understanding. These key possibilities of authentic assessment make it a prime assessment choice for the Transformative Learning Opportunities Model.

Portfolios

Portfolios take many forms and serve as valuable learning assessments within a framework of the Transformative Learning Opportunities Model. Two major formats include a developmental or longitudinal portfolio that chronicles the learners' development over a period of time and a final project portfolio that demonstrates the final product of the learners' work only. Both forms have their advantages. The developmental portfolio displays progression of work and development that show before and after skills and achievement. Additionally, this format enables educators to see what errors the learner might have made along the way and better chronicle formative development experiences. Such a representation is especially noteworthy in some cases, for instance when student progress is being used as a case study for teacher education, when the educator is required to enumerate the stages of development a learner progressed through during a course of study, or when significant progress is best demonstrated through actual representations of student work.

Additionally, portfolios can be used for professional or educational purposes as they present outstanding examples of student work across a variety of objectives, characteristics, skills, or competencies. In this way the final project portfolio provides a full-fledged professional product to use when the learner seeks job advancement, employment, admission to other educational programs, and in some cases completion of certification requirements.

Portfolios can be especially meaningful for documenting and facilitating transformative learning because they are holistic representations of learners' work. Portfolios can include self-assessment, through "entry" and "exit" reflections as examples of ways to demonstrate significant changes in understanding and meaning before and after learning experiences.

One of the strong points of portfolio assessment is the opportunity to build a case for validity. By collecting multiple samples of carefully designed student work, a holistic and valid assessment may be more possible than with a single, isolated sample (White, 1994). Portfolios may be assessed in many different ways including rubrics for content, composition, or format; individual and group/committee assessment; and contextual or positional assessment to name a few (Broad, 1994). Educators, learners, and/or other agencies or boards can assist in determining criteria and hence set the stage for reliability of the evaluation of portfolios. Usually in educational settings these criteria are delineated and distributed prior to learners creating their portfolio. Portfolios can have so many different forms from notebooks, to illustrations and technical drawings, to three-dimensional structures and for so many different purposes, as described above, that it is important to clearly specify the requirements and expectations beforehand. Such specifications will support reliable assessment by the educator (White, 1994).

Problem-based Learning

Problem-based learning is a different kind of authentic assessment. Rather than taking a test or writing a paper, usually problem-based learning will involve learners in solving a real-world problem or creating a project that addresses a problem and may cross content areas (Miller, 1998). Such learning activities can offer first-hand experience in a real or simulated setting that approximates the circumstances in which course content would be applied. Rather than separating knowledge or skills from application, learners are embedded in problems that can offer assessment of more complex cognitive and problem-solving processes.

Problem-based learning has long been used in professions like medicine, law, and business in the form of cases. Such cases provide realistic situations which students have to find accurate or viable solutions. Often these problems are complicated and multidimensional. Rather than situations that are easily solved, they can engage the learners in additional research, intense debate, construction of models or prototypes, simulations, or pilot tests.

Boud (in Miller et al., 1998) describes three major elements that need to be considered when assessing problem-based learning.

1. Careful specification of learning objectives and criteria is important for assessment.
2. Assessment is a process rather than a measurement activity.
3. Assessment is for the benefit of student learning. (p.182)

These points emphasize that problem-based learning closely weds student learning and transfer of learning. This makes problem-based learning particularly relevant to the Transformative Learning Opportunities Model because it allows the learner to join the instructor in stepping back from the learning experience and reflecting on meaning and form. Such reflection-on-action can provide a basis for learners to recognize changes and to delve further into the implications for themselves. Moving beyond accurate or correct responses, problem-based learning requires learners to evaluate a situation critically, determine a plan of action, execute it, and then have the result, and sometimes the process, assessed in order to further refine skills, insight, and application.

Collaborative Learning/Group Projects

A further variation of problem-based learning can be found in collaborative work. Many times, but certainly not always, group projects can be centered on a problem that needs to have a solution developed. Collaborative learning offers distinct benefits to transformative learning, as it requires learners to communicate in many ways and may require them to "participate in the co-construction of knowledge" (Peters & Armstrong, 1998, p. 75). For instance learners will need to articulate the project or problem at hand, assign responsibilities, communicate their ideas and opinions, participate in developing a solution, and come to an agreement about the final form and details of the project. Through all of these activities the learners encounter multiple viewpoints, experiences, and histories different from their own. They must communicate effectively and learn to negotiate solutions. Such challenges provide opportunities for understanding and adopting very different frames of reference –an environment readily consistent with transformative learning experiences.

Higher education students may be said to enthusiastically welcome group work (Miller, et al, 1998). However, there can be significant pitfalls that make some learners hesitant to enter into these projects. Sometimes group members ignore the opinions of others or do not fulfill their responsibilities. Group members can get very frustrated, although these difficulties can be learning opportunities if they are navigated successfully. For these reasons it is important that educators provide clear instructions and assessment criteria for the group project up front. Educators must also know how to cope with group dynamics and project problems. Finally, they need to apply the assessment criteria with a "reasonable degree of commonality of standards" (Miller et al., 1998, p. 164) so that assessment can be equitable across groups, therefore supporting its reliability.

The challenge of determining valid assessment of collaborative work lies in part with the activity instructions for assessment. Within the Transformative Learning Opportunities Model it would be possible to have the learners help decide on the criteria that they believe would identify fair assessment of the process. For instance they might choose to all share one grade or each person might receive separate and possibly different grades. They also can determine whether the assessment will be based on final performance, and/or contribution and whether group members will provide documentation or evaluation of their own and/or other group members' work. Collaborative learning can be an indispensable platform for student learning through planning instruction, reflection, and discourse.

Journaling

Journal writing is used in many settings to assist learners to capture their thoughts about the specific content area. Whether journals are kept online, in a notebook, or dictated, they serve the purpose of individual learners, usually, continuing to develop and analyze their thoughts beyond classroom dialogue (Hiemstra, 2001). As learners share self-selected portions of their journals with their instructors, further insight into their educational needs and development is gained.

Journaling can take many forms. Educators may provide structured reflective questions to guide learners to consider the readings or class lectures and discussion. Learners may take on a particular role for journal writing such as in role-playing or a simulation in order to think through situations and conflicts from a distinct perspective over time. For instance, teachers in training might keep a learning journal to explicitly focus on their role as a learner or middle management might engage in an extended simulation as a CEO of a business team and have to keep an account of the experience and dilemmas through a journal. Additionally, journals may be straight chronological accounts of learning experiences where learners debrief daily about their experiences in particular settings such as an internship, training program, or pilot project. In some cases journals may take more the form of logs where learners read materials and keep track of major points and their reflections reading by reading. An innovative form of journaling is the collective journal. Most likely facilitated through an online format, participants in a group project all participate at once or take turns creating journal entries for a group project.

Purposes for journals within the Transformative Learning Opportunities Model framework are many. At the same time that journals provide a running account of learner experiences, they can also serve as major vehicles for delineating, clarifying, and articulating understanding of the same. As learners work through conceptualizing the learner experience, thinking about its meaning, and drawing conclusions and implications, for instance, they are becoming critical thinkers day by day or week by week. They can explicitly practice and engage in reflective practice (Boud, 2001), which can be an effective facilitator of both ongoing lifelong learning and transformative learning.

Assessment of journal writing is challenging, but can be aligned with the purposes set forth for the activity. Working with students to delineate the scope and expectations of learning activities as well as the assessment facilitates greater understanding of learning that they may apply in a more self-directed form at a future time. As a specific example, when journals are evaluated on the basis of reflective thinking, different levels of reflective thinking can be identified (English & Gillen, 2001). Assessment of journals includes issues of confidentiality, potential retribution, and reliable, consistent measures through the use of rubrics or delineated criteria or standards (English, 2001). Having conversations with students about these issues will lead to the successful use of journals in assessing outcomes, some of which may indicate transformative learning.

A NEW VISION OF LEARNING

This chapter has considered the work of the educator within the Transformative Learning Opportunities Model. The work started with self-assessment, moved to planning instruction that facilitates trans-formative learning opportunities, and included designing assessment models and assessment learning activities. This discussion has extended our understanding of transformative learning to include different do-mains of learning such as cognitive, affective, and performance. Indeed, in order to embrace transformative learning and find meaning in our educational practice, we must develop a vision of learning in different domains.

Much has been written about learning in the cognitive domain; Bloom's taxonomy has become a standard in the education field (Sax, 1989). Bloom's categorization and organization of different thinking pro-cesses create a continuum from basic thinking skills such as understand-ing and comprehension to higher order thinking skills that include analy-sis and synthesis. And indeed many of our standardized tests measure achievement along this continuum. The transformative learning process certainly lends itself to Bloom's taxonomy as learners engage in critical thinking, analysis, and synthesis; however it is also much more. The general public and educators are well acquainted with learning as de-scribed by psychomotor performance when new skills and techniques are taught, and dexterity, ability, and performance are measured quan-titatively and many times qualitatively (for example, in some athletics). This understanding and experience open the door to reaching beyond the cognitive domain for our vision of learning. Therein lies a significant challenge for us as educators.

Transformative learning builds on the cognitive domain, but also frequently includes the affective domain. It is from this affective and cognitive perspective that we can approach reflective practice and self-assessment. Thinking about our work of teaching and learning, examin-ing our values and purposes, and extending our consideration of mean-ing and implications, are not purely cognitive endeavors. As compas-sionate, caring educators we enter into these considerations and deci-sions with our whole beings.

In this way, educators can catch a vision of teaching and learning that encompasses growth of understanding, development, and invention. Beyond performance alone, such learning taps the essence of our own and our students' generative abilities. This potential is demonstrated in the capability of adults to build on their history and experience and envision new possibilities. For many philosophers, this is the essence of the human spirit. A vision of casting our teaching and learning experiences within the greater realm of life and meaning brings a very different depth and dimension to our work as educators.

SUMMARY

The vision of reflective practitioners who begin instructional planning with self-assessment and focus on learner and organizational needs, is a vision of educators who see "the bigger picture" of their labors. Capturing the possibilities of transformative learning opportunities for ourselves and our learners, we begin an extensive, multilayered, and collaborative process of instructional design. Furthermore as we consider our growth and transformation, we also must confront our responsibilities as educators to assess student work that might depict transformative learning. In light of these dual emphases, this chapter provides extended consideration of reflective practice and alternative assessments and learning activities. It is a chapter that focuses on the educator. It focuses on our work of self-assessment and reflective practice that emphasizes our being and essence as adults and educators. It guides us to consider how to assess some indications of the transformative learning our students may experience. It leads to consideration of the larger questions such as: What is our vision for ourselves and learners? And how can we participate in bringing transformative learning to life?

CHAPTER 5

For the Learner: Keeping Supports Strong

A sea of change may surround adult learners who experience transformative learning. Change that opens new views, perspectives, and opportunities and change that brings an uncertain future are all possibilities. Learners can become engrossed in complicated changes. Transformative learning can include experiences that turn their worlds upside down. What they thought they wanted might vanish from their internal radar screen of values and aspirations. What they understood the world to be may metamorphosize into a bizarre and strange new reality. What they thought were their tried and true personal standards might turn out to be contradictions and result in escalating questions of value and worth.

Consequently this sea of change can turn into what some might consider negative or even disturbing change. Rather than bringing adults' worlds into an idyllic state of greater focus, purpose, and harmony, transformative learning can include drastic disruptions, even devastation. Crises of faith, confidence, and aspirations can be experienced. And even when learners resolve issues that may emerge in transformative learning experiences, their family, community, or workplace may not appreciate or tolerate the changes. When adult learners challenge their values, beliefs, and assumptions, they are often seen as challenging those of their family and community as well (King, 2003). Such circumspection and examination may not be welcomed as it puts others' convictions and assumptions at risk of exposure or contradiction.

Transformative learning is deep-seated change that may come at great cost to the learner. At the very least, learners experience the cost of letting go of the familiar and taking a risk on a new way of understanding. In worst case scenarios learners may be moving from a place of acceptance and support to one of separation or discipline. Given the analogy of transformative learning as a sea of change, it is clear that for many learners this sea is not one of steady, rhythmic waves lapping the

105

shoreline. Instead it may be more accurately visualized as a tumultuous sea where a storm is causing the waves to crash in many directions. The winds shift frequently, the water churns, visibility obscures, and moorings and anchors loosen.

This image brings to the forefront the urgent need to consider questions of support and even survival. In this complex transformative learning environment of competing values, expectations, and consequences, how can adult learners be supported? As learners critically consider questions of meaning, purpose, and the future, what is needed? When educators and learners value and desire such change, what do we need to provide or seek for our learners?

This chapter examines learner needs in the Transformative Learning Opportunities Model through the impact, ethical issues, barriers, and support related to transformative learning (Appendix A). The discussion of support focuses on educators and programs and considers what they may provide. The chapter concludes with three scenarios of dilemmas that educators and learners may encounter, thus illustrating learner experiences and needs that may eventually lead to transformative learning.

IMPACT

As adult learners navigate the sea of change of transformative learning, there can be many dimensions of its impact. Consequences and effects can emerge in many parts of their lives, including the personal, social, and professional. The changes are not confined to intellectual questioning, but can encompass emotions, physical safety, physical health, relationships, decisions, and actions. As illustrated in Figure 5.1 transformative learning can have a diffused pattern of impact on learners' lives.

Intellectual Questioning and Emotional Responses

Adult learners who experience transformative learning often experience affective results. The intellectual questioning they experience can reach into the inner being of the person. As they wrestle with issues of purpose and meaning, they challenge the core elements of themselves. Transformative learning usually is not a steady linear progression, but includes a deliberation of thought and action and a challenge of previ-

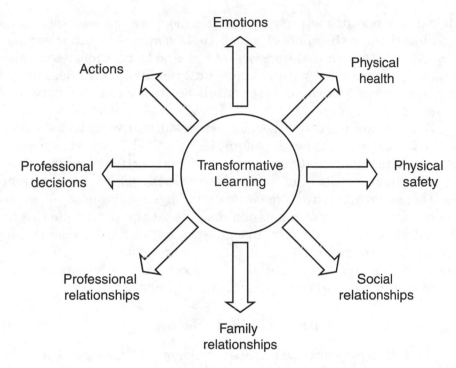

Figure 5.1 Transformative learning's impact.

ously accepted values and understandings. Building upon the essential element of dialogue among learners as they examine beliefs, values, and assumptions, we are reminded that learners engage in a potentially powerful and risky social/public dimension of their questioning. Through such a process of dialogue, reflection, and critical self-examination, learners may reach into intellectually and emotionally uncomfortable arenas.

Such critical questioning can bring with it self-doubt, fear, anger, or happiness. It can eventually emerge into confidence, but first needs to center on questions, examination, and inquiry. The travel route is not clearly marked here; instead the learner breaks a new path of personal understanding amidst crosscurrents of conflicting perspectives and possibly many obstacles. As learners question their values and understanding they may become fearful of the unknown, rejection, and loss. They may become angry with themselves or their communities because of their prior values and understanding as they examine them in new ways and find them lacking or wrong. They may become so awash in questioning that they are filled with self-doubt experienced in anxiety or depression.

Such learners may desperately try to find a mooring and seek something to stabilize them in the midst of intellectual turmoil. And other learners may question, discover new understandings, and be positioned to readily and happily embrace them. Intellectual questioning that plunges to core issues of meaning and value can certainly be an emotionally disruptive experience.

Understanding this dimension of transformative learning is critical in understanding the needs of adult learners. While we work to cultivate an environment that respects others' perspectives and views, we must also build a culture of questioning values, beliefs, and assumptions. These characteristics are foundational in developing self-directed learners capable of complex decision making. At the same time this intellectual approach of inquiry and questioning is tied to emotionally charged elements of identity, culture, social responsibility, and values, to name a few. The questioning needs to be recognized as having an affective impact that educators responsibly need to address.

Physical Well-Being

Learners may also experience extensions of these emotional consequences in their physical well-being. If they pursue such questioning, alone, in contradiction with their usual support communities, or drastically disrupting the grounding foundation of their lives, they may experience consequences in their physical health. Depression can emerge not only in emotional forms, but also in physical symptoms of tiredness, lack of energy, and bouts of tears. Continuous, sleepless nights spent deliberating on thoughts and choices and worrying about the impact of decisions can run down the physical health of learners. In extreme cases transformative learning could have such consequences.

In tandem with these deeply seated experiences, when transformative learning is disruptive to the social network of learners, physical safety may also be an issue. Questioning the status quo and raising provocative questions are not welcomed in all communities. In this light physical safety may be an urgent consideration. For instance when an abused spouse realizes she needs to take a proactive role in her life, change her understanding of herself, and stand against her abuser, physical safety is a major concern. Be it spouse abuse, political oppression, or many other stark manifestations of confrontation, such deeply rooted transformations of understanding may have physical consequences that cannot be ignored by educators and their organizations.

Social, Family, and Professional Relationships

To a less dangerous, but no less compelling, degree, social, family, and professional relationships may be greatly impacted as well. When adult learners question their personal and collective values and understandings, they bring other people and relationships into the consequences. Learners, who realize that they have the potential for greater learning and aspiration, may understand themselves in new ways. In so doing their understanding is communicated in their everyday relationships with others. It might be the wife who goes back to school, the 35-year-old man who moves out of his mother's house, or the line employee who takes steps to pursue a managerial position. Such decisions are not made in a vacuum. Instead learners interact with those around them in very different ways such as asserting independence, autonomy, or authority. The old rules of how husband and wife, mother and son, and employee and supervisor relate are called into question and relationships need to be explicitly or candidly renegotiated. Transformative learning is about critical questioning and working through the many manifestations of a person's being and experience. It will therefore swiftly impact how people relate with their world.

Actions

The decisions and actions that learners make through transformative learning experiences are the outermost manifestations of their learning and development. As intellectual questioning gives rise to new constructs and understandings, the final stages of perspective transformation necessitate decisions and outward change. New roles and decisions might be tested during the learning process, but the final stages include decisions for action and the reintegration of these new perspectives, through action, in their lives. Up to this point learners might have experienced the consequences of transformative learning in intellect and isolation. When they start making decisions and then put those into action, others can see evidence of the dramatic changes and learners are exposed. *When learners step into action they are poised on a precipice of risk.* At the same time that they look back and to the future, learners need to count the cost of their actions and plan for the consequences. Learners engaged in transformative learning are in great need of support in resolving these stages of learning as well. As learners take action on their learning, support is needed to withstand the consequences.

Oftentimes other educational theories and philosophies focus solely or mostly on cognitive change in this model; transformative learning includes the whole person — the mind, the body, and the soul. Reflecting on how transformative learning can impact learners' intellect, emotions, social relationships, and physical well-being illustrates the potential scope of such learning. While many consequences may be experienced while exploring the transformative learning journey, it is at the point of taking action that learners experience the major impact of the process and their decisions.

ETHICAL ISSUES IN SUPPORT

The risks that learners take in transformative learning start out as intellectual questioning and, as we have seen, ultimately result in actions that may or may not be accepted in the different circles of their world. Educators who facilitate transformative learning opportunities cannot ignore the risks that learners confront. Indeed examples of these risks and the need for support will be discussed later in this chapter, but for now let us turn our attention to issues of meaning and purpose.

When we as educators work with adult learners to promote critical questioning, issues of responsibility and ethics need to be raised and carefully considered. If we facilitate and encourage critical examination of values, beliefs, and assumptions, must we not be ready to support such questioning? In bringing transformative learning to life, learners engage in difficult experiences of questioning and examination. Do we as educators have the right to force them into radical change? From most philosophical and political stances, we certainly do not have the right to force them. Do we have a responsibility to introduce critical thinking, analysis, and more inclusive understandings of course content, themselves, and their world? From most perspectives, yes, we would want to cultivate lifelong learning, deep-seated change, and significant growth within our learners' experiences (Brookfield, 1987, 1990; Cranton, 1997; Mezirow, 1997; Mezirow & Associates, 2000). How then do we accomplish this while not forcing the hand of our learners?

Responsibility is a key concept in bridging these ethical questions. A primary component in facilitating transformative learning opportunities is for us to proceed with an open hand. In the same way that the Transformative Learning Opportunities Model is a dynamic and open-ended framework, so is our facilitation of these experiences. Whether in personal or professional issues, we as educators need to support a vision of possibilities, while also drawing attention to the costs and benefits of decisions that might be made.

A prime vehicle for promoting responsibility is for us to be upfront about intentions of learning activities and to include learners in instructional planning. Rather than any appearance of requiring radical change, the opportunities for transformative learning should be experiences that enable learners to critically question and dialogue and leave decisions for action in the learners' hands. Such planning has been termed "mindful" as educators consider learners' needs and contexts, the consequences of transformative learning for them, and the support that they are able and willing to provide (King, 2004a). Ethically, if we cannot provide support or any suggestions for resources, we must consider whether it is appropriate to introduce transformative learning. For some educators' educational and political philosophies and persuasions, it is consistent to do so regardless; others may consider it irresponsible.

The overarching recommendation is that in the midst of planning transformative learning opportunities, we need to be reflective practitioners (English, 2001). In this way the concepts of "mindful" planning and being "thoughtful" about the consequences of teaching and learning are manifested. When we look at adult learning as more than content and skill acquisition, we need to carefully consider the context, life, and needs of learners (King, 2004a).

BARRIERS

In considering the support that adult learners may need as they engage in transformative learning and their responsibilities, educators also become mindful of barriers learners may encounter. Major barriers to their transformative learning experiences can be viewed as internal or external.

Internal

Internal barriers are those which emanate from within the learners and may include their values, beliefs, fears, personalities, and learning styles to name but a few. If learners are deeply invested in their values and beliefs, the decisions, or even the consideration, of critical questioning could be a huge obstacle. Additionally, if learners are especially introspective, they might find this learning very comfortable. However if they are not used to introspection or are of an opposite inclination such as impulsive, the undertaking could be very difficult. Finally some people are distinctly independent in their learning; others thrive on the social communication aspects of learning. These different types of learners and personalities engage in transformative learning and related group activities in very different ways (Cranton, 1997).

External

External barriers to transformative learning can come from social or religious communities, governments, or families as a few examples. Such barriers might include explicit pressure to hold specific views without questioning or they might be more subtly enforced as certain mores or perspectives are supported and others are tolerated. When learners encounter external barriers to transformative learning, they need to determine how they will cope. This crossroads calls for a personal decision as to whether to continue along the path of critical questioning or to step aside from the journey. Will they challenge the external barriers, retreat, or delay? While learners might participate in a transformative learning opportunity in a class activity, they might not be invested or convinced of the need for questioning or change to be applied in their lives. External barriers can mean that learners have a great need for support, considering the significant changes they may experience in their understanding and their lives.

How then will we as educators deal with these barriers? The first point to consider is to realize that the decision to confront or accept any barriers rests with the learner. Next is to determine whether and what support we and our organizations can provide to overcome barriers that the learner chooses to challenge (King, 2004a).

Some barriers that face learners may exist in the educational environment. For example, if learners are uncomfortable sharing their opinions in large groups, we can try small groups. If learners find it difficult to understand what critical questioning is, we can provide additional experiences and examples to help them understand and practice the process. Nonetheless, some barriers are strictly outside of the classroom and learners need to find support to be able to challenge the barriers if they want to continue in transformative learning.

SUPPORT BY EDUCATORS

In prior research adult learners identified teachers, classmates, other students, advisors, and counselors as significant sources for support (King & Lawler, 1998). As students engaged in formal education and experienced transformative learning, the network of people they gained support from focused around that educational setting. This finding brings forth the necessity of considering how organizations, educators, and learners might or might not be prepared to provide support.

While the exact nature of the support the learners desired was not delineated, other studies have indicated that learners value dialogue, new insights, and additional resources during transformative learning experiences (King, 2002, 2003a). Indeed, teachers who are most familiar with and practice adult learning principles have been recognized by learners as most supportive (King & Lawler, 1998). Therefore educators can benefit from understanding the concepts and principles of this complex field and working to integrate them into their classroom practice. That is the major intent of the Transformative Learning Opportunities Model and this book. Indeed such responsibility should not rest with only those who have become familiar with transformative learning on their own; it should be shared across faculty and institutions. Informing our field of educators with this message and means of cultivating significant growth through supportive and facilitative learning environments can bring a powerful force to our systems and contexts of adult learning.

The educational environment should support questioning and reflective learning, and leave open options for learners to move into transformation at their own pace. Some learners may not take an explicit or public step during a course. Instead they may give thoughtful consideration to their choices and perspectives for an extended period of time. Educators who can cultivate an environment that includes safety, respect, and freedom can set the scene for learners to continue to engage in critical reflection of their understandings and their worlds.

Additionally, at this time learner-centered classrooms and active learning techniques are being more widely accepted in adult learning contexts, including higher education, community education, and some workplace settings. Therefore educators committed to adult learning might find a more receptive climate for their efforts (King, 2004a). Furthermore by bringing this perspective of the Transformative Learning

Opportunities Model into more organizations and settings, educators may also integrate transformative learning into the mainstream of educational practice and purpose. Preparation in the Transformative Learning Opportunities Model not only for faculty, but also for educational and psychological counselors and advisors within organizations can provide a broader base of understanding for transformative learning and the means to provide more visible and effective support.

Learners also identified classmates and other students as supporters of their experiences. Within this group, learners included support from students who might not have been in specific courses where they engaged in transformative learning. In the same way that the Transformative Learning Opportunities Model can be introduced to educators as an instructional design strategy, learners who engage in transformative learning opportunities as described herein gain experience in planning their own learning, critical questioning, and dialogue. These core elements can supply a dynamic base from which to build their own transformative learning and support such learning among other learners. Rather than classes and learning being teacher-centered, learners become the center for themselves and co-learners and supporters of others' experiences.

SUPPORT BY PROGRAMS

The need to provide support is naturally extended to what forms and kinds of support should be provided for adults engaged in transformative learning opportunities. Premiere in these recommendations are self-sustained support and access to additional resources.

Surely we cannot walk every learner through the entire transformative learning process as it unfolds in their lives in so many different dimensions. However, we can offer four major services to their learners:

1. Lifelong learning strategies
2. Listening
3. Dialogue
4. Evaluation

As learners engage in transformative learning opportunities, they gain valuable lifelong learning strategies and perspectives. As they assist in planning their learning, critical questioning, constructing new understandings, and developing applications of their learning, they move beyond dependency on a teacher for their learning. By introducing these major aspects of the Transformative Learning Opportunities Model into their educational practice, we provide self-sustained support that extends far beyond the specific time and place of the educational endeavor at hand.

Additionally, we as educators need to demonstrate key facilitation techniques by listening to learners articulate their questions and growing understanding and carefully probing their understanding and consideration with questions. As we engage in such interchange learners can gain valuable feedback about their thoughts and further encouragement to think about issues and implications they might not have considered previously. However we also must move these conversations into the peer-to-peer dimension, not only the teacher-learner relationship. Rather than building or maintaining an authoritarian relationship with the learner, these are opportunities to experience relationships with colleagues that include listening, understanding, and dialogue. It is critical that although this support might start with our learners and us that it extend beyond this relationship so that learners can see how to have continued support for the future.

In addition to lifelong learning, listening, and dialogue, developing a view of their world that incorporates critical questioning is a foundation for evaluation skills. Such skills are invaluable for learners throughout their lifetimes to make informed decisions about the deluge of information that adults face in their professional and personal lives (Mezirow, 1997).

Finally educators and their organizations need to consider what resources they can offer to learners as they experience transformative learning. Rather than focusing on resolving all the solutions to learners' needs in this extended and complicated learning experience, educators need to focus on providing broader resources that can be utilized beyond the classroom experience. In this light, we may work with our organizations to build resource lists and provide material for gaining additional information. Whether it is new housing, additional finances, a support community, or counseling, these lists can be used now and in the future to support study, understanding, and action. Some programs will be able to provide counseling on specific issues that may arise. However, there are certain to be times when the organization does not have counseling in a needed area, so that having resource lists to refer learners to additional and varied counseling services is a necessity. We as educators provide great support for our learners as we build experiences that incorporate lifelong learning, listening, dialogue, and evaluation. This support becomes centered in the learner as we facilitate their increasing self-directed learning.

Support from individuals and communities is critical. Educators and programs may encourage learners to build their own communities directly in their context. Or they can suggest resources to guide them to outside communities that can lead to steady, informed, and focused support in a specialized environment. For example, adults who are considering a dramatic change in their political understanding and affiliation would do well to gather information from a variety of sources about their options and to explore specific communities in which they would participate once those decisions are made. Guiding learners to discover resource organizations, services, and communities gives them valuable support systems for extending the classroom's effectiveness.

Transformative learning has so many implications and dimensions of impact that providing comprehensive support through a single organization is unrealistic. Instead, we and our organizations can focus on skills to provide support and resources for continuing learning and development beyond specific educational programs. From this strong base, learners can consider what other support might be needed, and whether and how it might be provided.

CLASSIC DILEMMAS

As we consider the implications for supporting transformative learning, at the same time that we plan and facilitate such support, our attention needs to focus on our learners' experiences and needs. By thinking through the needs of learners to cope with transformative learning, we can see vibrant ways in which this learning theory comes to life. Transformative learning can be experienced in an infinite number of ways and contexts. The following three scenarios are intended to expand our vision of possibilities across different learning contexts.

When adults return to higher education later in their lives, they often encounter very different concerns than more traditional adult learners might. Often in fact, they may already have encountered a disorienting dilemma, and this is the reason they have chosen to embark on the difficult road of balancing work, family, and formal education. However, for many learners the dilemmas, challenges, and related changes do not stop there. The first scenario depicts a returning adult learner who encompasses dilemmas within both the worlds of higher education and business.

Stephanie: Higher Education and the Workplace

Stephanie is enrolled in a human development class and is really cued into the different stages of adult living. Indeed, as she reads the material and discusses the case study with her professor and classmates, she begins to see herself through very different eyes. Prior to this class she has moved along life as it seemed to be planned; one opportunity always flowed to the next. Although her pathway to education has been along a unique timeline, she sees a natural and reasonable progression clearly enough. Yet as she reads the accounts of adults in their middle years reexamining their lives in light of the loss, tragedy, and assorted crises, she begins to reexamine her own life journey. Not knowing exactly how to chronicle her experiences, she finds the group project very helpful. The class has selected different groups and projects to participate in and her group is charting their lifelines individually and then integrating their separate experiences into a composite lifeline.

The group decides to graph their life events like a timeline with major events and stages marked clearly. The professor, Ron, meets with their group and listens to how they intend to pursue the activity. His suggestion is to include different opportunities, different ways, to think about and discuss their experience and insights. He also mentions that he is available as a resource to help on a group or individual basis. When the group meets the next time they have rough drafts of their work and share them with one another. It is surprising to Stephanie, but when she explains her lifeline, her classmates need more explanation in order to understand the events and how they transition from one to another. What is so obvious to her is not clear to others. Her classmates' questions help her think about new connections, explanations, and possibilities. She wonders about the direction her life is taking and her own values and life goals.

The group decides that they would each further refine their lifelines and write narrative accounts to explain them. As Stephanie begins writing, she thinks through the questions her group has been asking her. Why has she chosen business as a career? Why does she want to move into a management position in such a high-pressure field? What are the benefits for her, her family, and her career? And do the benefits outweigh the costs? Finally the most disturbing question that continues to circulate in her consciousness is – In her later years, when she looks back on her life, *what will she hope to have accomplished?*

Writing her thoughts about these questions helps Stephanie sort out her ideas and choices. In addition, the process raises several alternative choices for her. As she challenges the assumptions that have led her to this point in her life and career, she begins to realize that deep down inside she wants something more. She is not used to critically questioning her choices, let alone deep-seated values. Instead she has always been one to hear the call of duty or expectation and to step forward to perform as needed. Suddenly her world is taking a drastically different twist and she begins to look at truth and responsibility as constructs that can be questioned. She also catches a glimpse of the possibility that there may be many different truths and she can decide which one she wants to claim as her own and build upon. This perspective is an entirely different way of understanding truth, knowledge, and her life.

While she deliberates on these thoughts she tries to work out the possibilities on paper. She makes lists and determines priorities. These activities made it increasingly clear that business is not really her passion; it is instead what she has always felt she was expected to do.

At this crossroads she begins to take another vantage point and thinks about those dreams of teaching that she has always had. Stephanie remembers as a child playing school in the basement of her family home. She lined up her younger brothers and sisters at table and chairs and used a blackboard to teach spelling and math. She always enjoyed seeing them realize how to do something new and was very proud of the papers they did. Even at work she trains new employees often. The management quickly realized that she has a knack for explaining processes and procedures and that she is very supportive of other people's questions and needs to understand.

She goes to the next class—it is about six weeks into the project they are working on—and reads her narrative about her childhood dreams to her classmates. They look at her in silence for a few moments and then Charles says, "So what are you going to do?" Stephanie says what she knew had been deep inside but not voiced before, "I am going to pursue a teaching degree so I can work with adults who have had fewer opportunities than myself." Even as she says it for the first time, Stephanie knows this is her passion. Now lies the nearly impossible task of figuring out how to tell her husband that she is casting aside her 25-year business career and promises for a promotion, how to tell the boss who so trusts and mentors her that she is going to pursue this new career and eventually leave the company, and not least of all how to find and get admitted to a teaching program. She really does not know where to start. She feels she needs to start with those close to her, but this will be threatening to them as she undertakes a less secure and less lucrative professional path. The obstacles to her decision loom large before her. This new way of approaching her desires and future feels exceedingly strange. She is uncertain how to step forward into the empowered future she is creating for herself.

For a few days after that class session, Stephanie writes about these issues and implications in her journal, discusses difficult questions with her classmates, and finally decides to talk to Ron, the professor. She hopes to find out what counseling services or resources the school might have. She sends an email that describes the changes she is thinking about and some of the questions she has about her future. Ron emails back that night and is very encouraging of her revisiting her career and life goals. They schedule an appointment for later that week and Ron says that the university has both career and family counseling services available. Stephanie stops by the counseling center and picks up some materials before she visits the professor. Her discussion with Ron provides some insight into why people pursue teaching careers, what kinds of work they do, and which organizations employ adult educators.

After that session she returns to the center and asks for an appointment with a counselor that Ron has mentioned. The center offers individual counseling, testing, and discussion groups to help adults explore their career options, personality types, and occupational preferences. This is not a simple matter of changing careers. Stephanie wants to reevaluate her abilities, aspirations, and directions from a distinctly different perspective of independence and empowerment. Even though her final decision is not made and her problems not solved, Stephanie feels like she has people around her who understand these unsettling questioning experiences. She does not feel like it is odd at all to reconsider her career at 45 years old and she looks ahead at difficult choices, but with a sense that she is not alone.

Through her classes Stephanie has seen a disturbing dilemma form for her. As she learned of stages of adulthood and examined and discussed her own life course, she began to question her true desires and goals. Through dialogue with her classmates, she began to explore her true intentions and new possibilities. For her, the struggle included individual, family, and professional dimensions. There were difficult choices to be made, but she had begun to step forward as a self-directed and empowered learner to discover where this new understanding of herself would take her.

The next scenario reveals the experiences of an Eastern European immigrant woman who is taking ESOL classes. She encounters serious cultural and family dilemmas as she begins to pursue a career.

Alexandra: ABE and ESOL

As Alexandra enters the classroom she knows she is taking a momentous step. She has told her father she is taking classes so she can translate during his medical visits, but she knows she has other intentions as well. Alexandra's family and culture do not allow women to pursue careers. Yes, sometimes they have to work to supplement their family's income, but a career, a deliberate choice to pursue learning and economic independence, there is no place for this in her culture. Still, she enters the classes with a mixture of resolve and fear; she does not know what the outcome will be. Perhaps this program will not let her pursue a career either; maybe she is all wrong trying to grasp hold of her dreams and gain independence.

During the first class, the teacher, Abed, and learners introduce themselves by name and country of origin. Some of them can say more in English than others, but Abed helps the students learn how to express their goals for taking this class. The answers range from getting their first job in America, to changing careers, to being able to speak to their children's teachers, with many different purposes in between. Many aim to continue their education and work through the formal educational system to pursue college degrees here in the United States. When her turn comes she mentions how her father is sick and she needs to be able to speak to the doctor in English; she does not feel safe to publicly state her real reasons for being there.

Abed has many different activities for them to do that day. They learn English words for careers, employment, and business and practice using them in conversation and writing. The real surprise is that the time flies by because the students are so motivated to learn and the teacher has interesting activities. In these classes, sometimes they work from the blackboard sometimes they work with a partner, and other times they are in groups discussing the possible meaning and use of words that they choose to research. Alexandra is not used to working with classmates at all or to the unusual way Abed interacts with their ideas and learning needs. Instead of saying, "Here is the list of what we are going to do" the students have choices and make decisions about their learning together as a group! All the while Abed visits the different groups to see if they have questions, need resources, or have any difficulties. They are on their own, but feel they have a caring and wise help line close by.

By the third week, Alexandra knows she is going to meet her friends each day she goes to class. Even though they are from different parts of the world, those in the group she works in the most know a lot about each other and help each other with class work. In their class they are not just studying English vocabulary and grammar, but they use the language in all its different forms as they talk about their experiences. At different times they talk, write about their thoughts or discussion, or take notes about what Abed or their classmates say. Yet throughout all the activities there is a definite feeling of warmth, understanding, acceptance, and dedicated study. Early on Alexandra realizes that these are people she can trust and that they think her opinions and ideas are valuable. She is an independent individual supported by friends who care when she enters this room.

One day she decides it is time to truly reveal to her classmates why she wants to learn. This is an environment where she is respected and she feels pretty certain that if any group of people could accept her dreams, this would be the one. Today the learning activity is to talk about what they want to do in the future. Where would they live? What would they do? Alexandra knows the time has come to share her secret. With trembling and sweaty hands Alexandra speaks when it is her time to share. She stumbles a little at first and then begins to talk about people working in hospitals. She talks about taking her father to the hospital every week and seeing how the nurses and doctors are so critical to his medical progress. She then takes the very bold step and says that she wants to become a doctor too. She stops after that statement and her classmates look at her expectantly. Elsie asks how much schooling that takes in the United States. And Marco asks if she has worked in a hospital. None of them are shocked; none of them are distressed that she desires to pursue such a radical dream. As they talk more they also ask why she looks so surprised and she says it is because she is scared and that people will be furious about her career goals. Then a knowing look comes over the faces of a few of them. She also tells them that she has wanted to study for this career for a long time, but has never been able to until the need came for her to intervene in her father's healthcare.

During the coming weeks, Alexandra speaks with her classmates often about her medical career dream. She finds they ask her difficult questions about her academic preparation, her family's response, and her reasons for wanting this career. She finds she has to dig deeply into and examine her basic values and beliefs to build the full answers she needs. She also finds her classmates supportive. One of them has a sister who is a nurse and offers to have Alexandra over for lunch to talk about how she might get a job in a hospital for some work experience. So the career aspect of the plan is moving ahead, but she has not dealt fully with the family relationships and dynamics yet.

That week Abed has the students begin to keep a journal about their daily learning experiences. This is a challenging activity because even though they are moving into intermediate levels of English learning, keeping a daily journal includes a lot of vocabulary. Through the journal she describes how she is learning about the medical field from her friend's sister and the many trepidations she has about telling her family about her career choice. However, she states she knows the time is quickly approaching when she will have to do it. She even asks Abed if there is any help for women who go to school. The teacher talks with her after the next class and invites her to come during office hours to talk about her educational goals whenever she feels she is ready and if she thinks he can be of assistance.

Alexandra takes him up on the offer about a month later, because when she finally tells her family, her father explodes in anger. Alexandra is given an ultimatum either to stop taking classes immediately or to leave the house permanently. Surprisingly, she is not in too great a panic because she had expected this might happen and has been looking at ads in the local paper for roommates. What she wants to know from Abed is whether she has demonstrated the ability to go to college and later medical school. When they meet that morning before class, Alexandra frankly asks him about her academic performance. Does she show enough ability in English learning? Does she seem like a student who will be able to go to college and earn a degree? Abed tells her that she has in fact excelled very rapidly in the classes and that her English learning and, as communicated in her writing, her way of thinking and reasoning are certainly on the level of those who go to college. He also tells Alexandra about the placement exams they will take next month and what she needs to score to realistically consider college application. It turns out the program also has an occupational resource center that Alexandra has not known about and that a resource person can help her look up local colleges, entrance requirements, college transcript translations, and academic requirements for various medical careers. There are many possibilities and based on her performance this year it appears that Alexandra will find many op-

portunities suitable for her level of ability. Alexandra also brings up the family and housing issues as informational points and Abed asks if Alexandra knows for certain this is what she wants to do. Alexandra says that she has wanted it for so long, and feels so unfulfilled in her current life, that she knows this is the path she needs to take.

With its difficult changes and risks in family relationships and physical well-being, this is a story that is lived by many learners in diverse educational settings. They catch a vision of a dream, plan their course, bide their time, and gradually move ahead to difficult decisions and, sometimes, breakages. While Alexandra certainly came to the learning situation with her vision in mind, it was through the experiences of respect, trust, and dialogue that she continued to move forward. This was an experience of transformative learning happening over a long period of time. There was no flash of a disorienting dilemma. Indeed the ongoing desire to pursue an unacceptable career path was the problem that this experience centered about. The learning experiences furthered the process; they fed the understanding of the issues, possibilities, and consequences. They supported the need to work though the possibilities and develop a plan in confidence and time. Alexandra's way of understanding her choices about her career and family evolved through the learning process. She separated cultural and personal expectations and realized a significant shift in her sense of self as independent and validated. Alexandra moved through the process and took the final steps of breaking with her family expectations and traditions. She took responsibility for her actions and began creating a future for herself that was rooted in her newly clarified values and goals. Through hard decisions and much sacrifice, she had created a new future.

The final scenario is one taken from faculty learning experiences where professors are learning web page development. Such learning can be problematic for some professors because they are used to being experts or need to project an expert status in their fields. Therefore taking on the role of the novice can be very distressing. The difficulties that may arise give substantial reason to support faculty as they take the risk to admit their need for learning and pursue it in a public setting, such as a class.

Jennifer: Faculty Development
Jennifer is finally ready to make the leap. She is fast on the course of fulfilling tenure requirements at this major university through her new

research project. However she desperately needs to be able to post find-
ings during the project on her own web site. As required by her funder, the
project is such that while the funds are adequate to support the research,
they do not leave enough to include paying someone for doing these fre-
quent web page updates. To this end, she enrolls in the "First Things
First" web page development workshop series on campus.

Jennifer is surprised to see several faculty from her school in the
university-wide workshop. She has mixed feelings about that develop-
ment. She is a junior faculty member, so not many faculty in the other
schools know her. And her philosophy is to keep a low profile, so she has
hoped to slip in somewhat anonymously. However that plan vanishes when
she walks into the crowded classroom. She is deeply conflicted because
she needs to learn, but does not want to be known as less than an expert.
As a professor she is supposed to have all the answers, isn't she? And here
she feels like a novice. In fact she has delayed taking any professional
development, because of this fear. Now she is distressed with the conflict-
ing needs for learning and protection.

However, when she starts talking with Lesley, the chemistry pro-
fessor sitting next to her, she learns that all of the faculty in the workshop
are in the same situation she is – they need to learn. Indeed, how different
is this when compared to her own learners? Many of them are highly
respected professionals in their fields, and yet they are taking undergradu-
ate courses to complete a degree that most of their colleagues have done 20
years earlier. In fact, we all have things to learn in different parts of our
work and lives. Maybe this class will offer more than web page develop-
ment skills to her self-understanding.

Thankfully, the professional developer, Naomi, is not only a tech-
nical guru, but also evidently a master teacher. Jennifer is surprised at
the many different activities in which they engage. Who would have
thought group learning fit into computer classes? Indeed, early on Naomi
makes it clear that she wants them to be a learning cooperative. But,
Jennifer thinks, if she works with other faculty they will see how much
she does not know! She will be exposed and she will have lost control.
However Naomi's style is that rather than isolated "silos" of learning, she
talks about and builds groups of professors to work on projects together.
In fact they deal with controversial topics that explore greater issues of
web design and teaching and learning. Rather than just learning the
mechanics of the software programs needed to do the task, they critically
evaluate other websites, discuss the issues and implications of the dispar-
ity of computer and Internet access across race, gender, and socioeconomic

lines (the digital divide), and consider whether and how they can use some of these teaching techniques with their own learners. This is a much more intellectually stimulating experience than she expected. She finds she is reexamining her purposes and conceptions of teaching and learning and is questioning her understanding and beliefs about her role as a junior faculty member.

Naomi's short series of workshops also feed into several enduring support systems. In addition to more advanced workshops, one-on-one support is available in the walk-in faculty instructional technology center, frequently asked questions (FAQ's) are posted on the web in a searchable database, a faculty web development listserv is available, and lunch meetings are held every two weeks that discuss not only technology but also faculty career issues. This is a community of people and services that understand the academic responsibilities, demands, constraints, and culture in which they work. It is a welcome community of peers to have found while she is on what has been a lonely and difficult road to tenure. Her vision of a divisive, competitive faculty has been more fear than reality. The support services and community create an entirely different view of her work and her learning needs.

The disorienting dilemma for Jennifer is how to cope with these roles that are conflicting for her. She is teacher and learner, academic expert and technology novice, all rolled into one person. Sometimes the emotions are quite confusing because she is still fighting off the fear that she might be "exposed" to her students or colleagues as less than an expert in anything. However as she engages in the variety of activities of the workshops and the technical and academic support system, she begins looking at the role of the professor in a different way. Sometimes the faculty lunch sessions are about teaching and learning issues and how if we as educators value the experience of the learner, we can incorporate this through dialogue or testing or group work. The professors discuss, disagree, and search for more inclusive perspectives as they wrestle with such timely questions. In the midst of this learning Jennifer sees that many of her colleagues are quite comfortable being learners. The fact that they do not know answers to all these thorny issues that are raised week after week does not really bother them. They just use their skills of research, analysis, and dialogue to work through new understandings.

Jennifer gains much more from these introductory workshops than web page design. Instead, she begins to create new expectations for the professor she is becoming. Rather than falling into the stereotypes she had developed over her student academic career, she is part of a commu-

nity of learners who explore issues, collegially wrestle together over mean-
ing, and create new understandings. She begins to see knowledge as con-
structed rather than only transmitted. She begins to see she needs to reex-
amine her personal and professional values and beliefs. The opportunity
to grow in this new way of being and understanding is in her hands. She
is catching a vision of a very different future for herself. Many of the par-
ticipating professors have gained new understandings of specific topics;
Jennifer has started to build new understandings of herself and the roles
she chooses to invent for herself.

Jennifer enabled the professional development workshops to reach
to core issues of her personal and professional identities. Finding herself
in a threatening position she evaluated the situation, considered her
options, and chose to step forward into the risks that were ahead. For
her, these beginning steps of transformative learning were primarily
personal perspectives of her expectations and herself. She wrestled
through them and it is likely that working through them in action will
be a continuing experience. Transformative learning does not provide
crisp clean solutions. This experience reaches into the core issues and
understanding of learners. It opens new possibilities.

NOT FACING THE OPEN DOORWAY ALONE

The message of this chapter is that adult learners should not be
facing the journey of transformative learning alone when they are engaged in organized transformative learning opportunities. By being aware
of the experiences of such learners, we and our organizations can better
understand students and prepare for their support.

Transformative learning experiences certainly are not always idyllic journeys to new ways of understanding. Instead they can be complex
experiences because both their roots and impact are far-reaching. Transformative learning changes can include learners' family, friends, work,
and politics. Through changes come greater freedom, responsibility, distress, confidence, confrontation, happiness—the whole range of actions
and emotions. Adults will find this type of learning in many parts of
their lives. By experiencing it through thoughtful learning activities in
an environment of safety, respect, and support, they can gain the advantage in better understanding and navigating the dramatic changes that
can accompany it. Understanding this complexity is contingent on un-

derstanding the many different learners and their infinitely different contexts.

SUMMARY

This chapter has suggested some significant ways educators can conceptualize the impact, issues, responsibilities, and possibilities of support:

- Create a class climate of safety, respect, and freedom.
- Cultivate a vision of and skills for lifelong learning.
- Support critical questioning, dialogue, and new perspectives.
- Link learners to organizational resources.
- Make students aware of referral services to additional organizations, services and communities.

We emphasize that the focus of the Transformative Learning Opportunities Model, especially when we consider support, is on the learner. We as educators can create transformative learning opportunities, but the decision and responsibility to pursue that pathway of significant change of understanding, perspective, and meaning making remain with the learner. Through the scenarios and discussion, this chapter brings more of the realities and possibilities of transformative learning to life.

CHAPTER 6

Looking Forward: Imperatives for Action

The vision of future research and development can lead to generating many new possibilities for the theory and practice of transformative learning through the work of classroom educators, adult learners, and researchers alike. Rather than a static instructional regimen, the Transformative Learning Opportunities Model is dynamic and serves many diverse teaching and learning needs. The model shows the way to facilitate transformative learning opportunities so that, ultimately, theory may come to life in the lives of adult learners.

USING THE MODEL

Here is a vision of adult learning that at once focuses on the experiences of the learner, delineates the work of the educator, and integrates the specific context of learning. Shown in Appendix A, Figure 2.1, the Transformative Learning Opportunities Model is a semistructured yet dynamic framework that reaches beyond a linear progression of instructional design or planning. Instead, the emphasis is on its key elements: the interdependence of the stages, the critical and generative participation of the learners, and the integration of specific organizational, community, and content needs, constraints, and contexts. This open-ended design allows all of these voices and factors to participate in creating experiences that may lead to transformative learning.

Walking Through the Model

Jamal's story from Chapter 2 is an extended example that reminds us of one possible learner's experience in the Transformative Learning Opportunities Model. Illustrated in Appendix A, Figure 2.2, the model encompasses a pathway of experience that includes building safety and trust, determining needs and expectations, creating learning experiences, and revisiting needs, teaching, and learning. While these stages in the pathway are represented in a sequence, the discussion reveals that they are part of an interdependent, fluid progression. The learning experiences are more specifically delineated as engaging in critical reflection, cultivating dialogue, and envisioning and supporting application. In a constantly evolving context and format, learners critically evaluate their values, beliefs, and assumptions. Pushing at the edges, as we have described, learners ask deeper questions such as these:

- Why do I think the way I do?
- Why do I cling to certain assumptions?
- What do my past experiences mean?
- What do I value?
- What do I desire for my future?

Cultivating the perspectives to examine familiar principles and values critically through introspection and then dialogue gives adults the skills to continue lifelong learning independently. They become familiar with the strategies to support self-directed learning. The groundwork is laid for continued development, learning, and action far beyond an individual workshop, course, or classroom.

As Jamal's trainer, Jacqueline, worked with him, she demonstrated many aspects of the educator's work described in Layer 2 of the Transformative Learning Opportunities Model. As illustrated in Appendix A, Figure 2.3, we as educators are active in self-assessment, preplanning research, and practice. These three stages are filled with not only activity but also fundamentally critical thought and planning. In self-assessment we examine reasons for teaching in general and for the specific initiative or content area at hand. This can include journal writing and discussions with colleagues. Hopefully collegial relationships, professional reading, educators' classroom experiences, and professional development opportunities will feed the fires of reflective practice. Preplanning research is also started before the learners arrive. This is the time to investigate needs, objectives, achievement, prior knowledge and skill, and prior learning experiences. The goal is to prepare preliminary instructional plans that are consistent with the specific learners and context.

While both of these stages are intensively active in thought, analysis, and research, the practice stage brings our work into another dimension entirely. Now we join with the learners to do the following:

- Determine learners' individual and collective needs and objectives.
- Facilitate learners' planning of instructional activities action plans.
- Continually assess learners' progress and needs.
- Effectively guide learners to resources that will support and extend their learning.

This practice stage intertwines with Layer 1, the learners' experiences, as the preparatory work of the educator leads into the developmental, collaborative learning process. At the same time, we continue self-assessment and research while the actual learning experiences are in progress. These dynamic processes can navigate the many needs, obstacles, and opportunities that arise during active experiences of transformative learning. Not confined to a preset agenda, the Transformative Learning Opportunities Model facilitates a context in which learning experiences may evolve that challenge and meet the diverse needs that arise in adults' increasingly complex, multidimensional lives.

The model traces these two layers of experience and yet as illustrated in Appendix A, Figure 2.4, it overlaps and revisits the stages continually. For instance, while the educator is planning, the learner is still growing, and while educators will be working with the learners to identify their current needs and objectives as they dialogue, learning is even then beginning to take place. The principles, activities, and players interweave into a composite that is dynamic and meaningful because of the potential each individual brings to the experiences.

Together these strands of experience and practice may interweave to be something much greater than their individual parts. At those times when the educator, learners, and environment mesh and learning opportunities begin to move toward experiences of transformation, something much greater begins to happen. When learners begin to look at their ways of understanding in significantly new ways, when they begin to question their cultural and contextual experiences, which can include their values, beliefs and assumptions, something powerful is unleashed. Learners experiment with new views and deliberate on what fits their future comfortably. And ultimately, learners may choose to transition into this new perspective and leave behind their prior understandings.

Looking at the Process

Such changes are significant learning and life-changing experiences. These are much more than an intellectual assent to new concepts and ideas. These changes strike at the core of the adult learners' being, at their way of understanding their world and translating their purposes and meaning into their everyday lives. In the words of Mezirow, transformative learning is about developing new meaning structures that fundamentally reframe adults' meaning making.

Inherent in such fundamental change are many toll-taking risks. Change that shifts the fundamental framework of learners' understanding does not happen silently or invisibly, at least not for long. For example, as adults reexamine their cultural values in the light of other cultures and perspectives, they might see serious shortcomings. Through learning experiences they may come to understand other views and choose another belief system. While this is important for their individuation and development, there can be a heavy personal cost. Those who belong to the original cultural community might not embrace, or even more strongly reject, their transformation. It is not unusual for adult learners who take such steps to be ostracized or rejected by their communities. Yet, based on my research and experience, adults take the conscious step into such dramatic change because either they can no longer embrace their prior ways of understandings or they catch a vision of the possibilities ahead or both. I believe there is great personal power embedded in these experiences. It certainly does not reduce the risk, fear, or, at times, anguish, but it demonstrates necessary responsibility and potential power of the adult learner.

In other instances perspective transformations can be powerful positive experiences where change is embraced by those around the learner and new pathways of opportunity unfold. Adults see themselves in new ways and gain new confidence in themselves as their prior experience is validated. They discover their greater intellectual abilities, and move ahead powered by their desires and vision. The ABE learner, Isabel, in Chapter 1, is an example. Although she had never succeeded in educational pursuits before, she completed her program and gained confidence in herself as a learner and a member of her community. That we as educators can be some small part of providing a seed of understanding, opening a doorway, or offering support is a large responsibility. The Transformative Learning Opportunities Model is our guide.

NEXT STEPS—IMPERATIVES TO ACTION

As educators we need to consider how to put the Transformative Learning Opportunities Model into action. Although there are many ways to approach this challenge, building on the framework of the model I suggest three preliminary steps that may guide educators: self-assessment, understanding learners needs, and understanding organizational context, climate, and culture. This brief action plan will be the foundation for pursuing the model's framework in-depth and operationalizes the basis for educators' pursuit of the model in theory, principle, and practice.

Self-assessment

The first action is to engage in reflective self-assessment. We as educators need to consider our own educational philosophy – our understanding of the adult learner, our purposes for being an educator, our goals and objectives in teaching and learning, and our beliefs, asking, Where am I in my thinking about adult learning? Why do I do what I do as I prepare for and engage in teaching? What do I expect or hope to happen through participants' learning experiences? We can revisit our focus, goals, and objectives for adult education in general and then gradually move to the learners and the setting in which our next initiative will take place.

Building on this assessment and clarification, we need to address the issues of ethics and responsibility. How does transformative learning and what I do in the classroom interrelate and impact the learners' larger community? How will learners cope with change? How will they deal with oppression? What barriers will such learners face? How will learners shoulder responsibility? Will they be prepared to do so through these experiences or their prior background and resources? What is ethical? What is my responsibility?

As demonstrated in Chapter 5 these questions bring forth issues of support for learners. We educators need to think about how to plan instructional experiences and support learners in discovering their pathways should they embark on a transformative learning journey. Thinking through these questions of responsibility and support from the beginning brings the reality of transformative learning experiences to the forefront. Transformative learning can have far-reaching implications and impact for learners and organizations. Hence we as educators bear responsibility not only in cultivating lifelong learning, but also in supporting deep change within the lives of our learners.

Our self-assessment can take place, for example, through a reflective journal, dialogue with colleagues, an electronic bulletin board, or correspondence. Such efforts can serve to reach within and beyond ourselves to understand better our goals and responsibilities in teaching and learning. Thinking about the hard questions that surface with transformative learning, we must not be afraid to press further and question whether and how such learning fits. We need to not cast transformative learning aside as too risky or apart from the programmed curriculum, but look to see where the skills and experience of critical thinking, self-directed learning, and collaboration can interplay to effect positive, lasting experiences for our learners now and in the future.

Furthermore, transformative learning does not have to happen in our classrooms. Instead the transformative learning opportunities can serve as dormant seeds to be cultivated much later in an individual's life. We do not know where individual learners are along a continuum or pathway of transformative learning; oftentimes they do not know either. But their engagement lays the groundwork for substantial learning and new thinking about experiences, beliefs, and assumptions that can be invaluable. Such experiences can cultivate a critical perspective, an informed citizen, and a wiser parent, spouse, and consumer. It is empowering when learners can evaluate information in light of their frame of understanding and are able to pursue its meaning and application for themselves. Whether that happens now or somewhere in the distant future is nearly irrelevant. It is the process and the paradigm of substantial challenge, change, and construction that is the essence of the Transformative Learning Opportunities Model. Reflecting on these greater purposes and effects through self-assessment provides deep roots for our teaching.

Understanding Learners' Needs

The next area that flows from this self-assessment is that of understanding learners' needs. Rather than designing solely an isolated expert-centered agenda for learning and instruction, we need to research what, in this specific context and initiative, are the needs and objectives of the learners.

Focusing on the adults with whom we will work, turns attention on the needs, context, and prior experiences that they bring with them to the learning experiences we will plan and facilitate. Adult learning principles are the guide here.

- Recognize, validate, and utilize prior experience.
- Engage learners in active learning.
- Utilize collaborative learning.
- Identify application for learning.

As educators consider these principles, questions will surface about prior experiences, desires, inclinations, and abilities that learners may have. Understanding whether they have had positive or negative past learning experiences in these settings is critical to preparing the tone and climate for the initiative. Exploring learners' prior experiences and preferences for active and collaborative learning can guide our thoughts as to viable instructional strategies and how much preparation the learners will need. Finally, understanding whether learners are comfortable with application of their learning and knowing their expectations and needs lay the groundwork for a learner-centered focus to our instructional planning.

Understanding learners' needs for content and operational learning leads us to an even more focused point of instructional planning. In this action plan it is paramount to move from self-assessment and strategic planning to the specific learner needs that have to be addressed. In some settings these are clearly predefined as the learning initiative may be interrelated to other courses of study. However in most settings there is room to negotiate additional objectives and that can build learner-identified needs while also moving toward possible transformative learning. Learners who engage in activities that address their current needs can be highly motivated to explore how and what to learn. Tapping into this motivation and investment of effort can be a powerhouse to support active, meaningful, and thoughtful transformative learning.

In preplanning efforts educators can work specifically to unearth these needs. Asking questioning about current conditions and future expectations can develop these considerations further and explicitly. What do the learners need to be able to understand and do as a result of these learning activities? How might lifelong learning and transformative learning be valuable goals for these learning initiatives? Where will they be called upon to apply their learning? What is the timetable for them to accomplish this goal? How will their efforts and accomplishments be evaluated and measured? What voice do they have in developing new objectives and refining preexisting ones? What are their needs for motivation, instructional support, and resources? What is available to them? Are there any learning disabilities or barriers that might be encountered? How would these be identified and what corrective or assistive measures will be available? What existing needs for voice and participation in learning do learners already have? These questions focus on the learner and yet are cast within the context of the organizations where they working or learn. Exploring this context further is critical in completing our initial action plan.

Understanding Organizational Context, Climate, and Culture

Early on in our thinking we need to consider the context, climate, and culture within which our learners will apply their learning. Questions include, As far as I know at this time what are the goals and needs of the learners within the organization involved in this learning initiative? What would transformative learning and lifelong learning mean and how would it be experienced in this context? What elements of the model might fit this context? What elements might not? In what ways would the organization benefit from this perspective? How can transformative learning be introduced as a means or framework for lifelong learning?

Additionally, we as educators need to consider the extensive implications and impact of potential transformative learning. What it will mean for learners as they return to their organizations, social, religious, and family networks? Such deep-rooted significant change impacts many aspects of learners' lives and the responsible educator must be aware of the implications of this learning. What support can we and our organizations offer if transformative learning is experienced? How will we support critical questioning? What options may be available? How do we leave the door to transformative learning opportunities open to learners without conscripting their participation? What does it mean for me to be a responsible educator in this context? Are these experiences possible or contradictory? And if it will be a very difficult fit for learners and myself, what are the costs?

Often adult educators work with learners and the relationship is discontinued sometime afterward. So, the responsible educator needs to think about when the learners return to their specific working and personal contexts. If they have experienced transformative learning, will they be welcomed, tolerated, or rejected? Will they have community support or will they be on their own? And the summarizing question is, What are the consequences of transformative learning for these learners in these contexts?

Educators would do well to gather information preliminarily about the environments to which learners will return and the expectations, climate, and cultures embedded within them. Including these considerations even in initial planning creates a much more accurate, complex, and representative picture of the whole learner and prepares a pathway of responsibly pursuing use of the Transformative Learning Opportunities Model.

The emphasis is on careful assessment and questioning concerning the purposes of the educator, and the needs and contexts of the learners. By gathering data and giving careful thought to these considerations, educators can pursue application of the Transformative Learning Opportunities Model. Keeping the focus on persons rather than solely on content acquisition provides a foundation for learning that can change the lives of all involved. Rather than meeting the requirements of a discrete goal or objective, the model provides a basis for introducing or further developing skills of and a vision for lifelong learning.

VISION OF FURTHER RESEARCH AND DEVELOPMENT

This book is a guide to how we can bring transformative learning into practice and what it means within our many contexts of adult learning. As educators explore the details of this model, it is intended that new development and directions will spring forth. As new experiences and perspectives emerge, our understanding of transformative learning theory, research, and practice will grow as well.

Research of transformative learning should not be delegated or left to academia alone. Instead adult education programs and educators need to proactively engage with colleges and universities to partner in their research inquiries and also engage in action research of their own.

Quigley and Norton (2003) and others (Mills, 2000) delineate empowering examples of practitioners pursuing understandings and solutions to the practical challenges of teaching and learning.

Educational research does not have to be abdicated to academia. Concepts and models of research can be empowering to practitioners. They may delineate teaching and learning needs, pose questions to investigate, and explore solutions. While these efforts might be pursued through traditional highly quantitative and experimental forms, they do not have to be confined to such paradigms. Instead educational research can include problem solving and exploratory endeavors. Action research and hypothesis-generating research are two examples that will be discussed here.

First of all, a basic research framework includes problem, method, data gathering, analysis, and application. This simple outline starts with educators considering the issues, or preliminary issues, they desire to pursue. Such questions as follows begin to explore the multitude of possibilities that are within our experiences of teaching and learning daily. What problems emerge in my classes? Where do my learners need more help? How can my instructional plans be improved? What are the results of using specific instructional strategies? After the question or problem is identified, a systematic approach to gathering data is the next step.

Research methods serve to delineate a systematic approach to gathering data for specific study. As educators we can explore many possibilities, but approaches that are especially useful in classroom settings include case studies, action research, and mixed methods. Data gathering can be conducted through observation, interviews, surveys and questionnaires, focus groups, and assessment tools, to name a few methods. These data gathering methods can be used individually or two or more can be used for the same project. Several resources provide clear explanations of why and how different research and data gathering methods might be used (Creswell, 2003; Gall, Borg, & Gall, 1996; Mills, 2000; Morse & Richards, 2002; Nardi, 2002; Yin, 2003). We need to carefully consider which methods and strategies fit the questions and problems we are approaching rather than which methods we might prefer or find easiest. Carefully matching methods to the problem is an important step that might benefit from consultation and collaboration with other educators.

Once a method and strategies are decided upon, we begin to gather data. This can take a day or two or it could take months, depending on the scope of the project and the research questions or problems that are pursued. Additionally, delays and complications in using strategies and gathering data emerge and these can prolong the timeframe. However time spent gathering data is well invested as these data will be the heart of the research project.

As the data are finally gathered and reviewed, educators begin analyzing it. For data gathering tools such as questionnaires and objective tests, frequencies, variances, and percentages can serve as preliminary analyses followed by statistical calculators to explore relationships among variables and predictors of future behavior. For qualitative studies of observations, interviews, and focus groups, educators may read and classify the findings to determine themes that tie together commonalities and eventually delineate differences among responses and experiences. Analysis is not an easy task. Educators may ask colleagues to help in examining the data and exploring how to analyze and make meaning of the findings.

The last step in many classroom research projects is to take the analysis of the data and see how it applies to the classroom. Educators will want to step back a bit from the data and consider how it fits into other perspectives of the same issues. Does it support other theories and practices? Does it demonstrate new ideas and needs? What does it mean for how I approach instructional needs? What limitations would there be on applying these findings beyond my specific context? These are all valuable questions that can guide consideration of the data for meaning and application.

Beyond the classroom dimensions of research, educators should also consider how to share the results. It might be giving a brief report to the teaching team, program, or organization. Perhaps we could submit a report or summary to an educational newsletter or journal in our field. Maybe there would be opportunities to present our study at a local, regional, or national conference. More than sharing what educators find in the classrooms, many of these possibilities include the potential to extend the educators' understanding, analysis, and application further as others interact with them about it. Through such research, we have the opportunity to develop new directions and possibilities for teaching and learning and, more specifically, our understandings and applications of transformative learning.

NEW POSSIBILITIES

The Transformative Learning Opportunities Model is not a final, universal instructional roadmap. Instead it is a dynamic, flexible, and generative framework to guide us as educators as we consider, plan, and facilitate transformative learning opportunities across our many contexts. Taking a highly theoretical learning concept to the reality of instructional application is a tall order, but it holds immense possibilities for the field.

As we experiment with this approach at the classroom level, we might ask, What are additional needs of these learners that should be considered? What might transformative learning look like in these settings? How can educators consistently identify it in this context? What instructional and planning strategies seem promising to explore for transformative learning opportunities? What additional strategies will meet the needs of these learners?

From a broader level of the theory of transformative learning, our classroom research might offer the field new considerations. Are there certain types of transformative learning that we can identify within or among contexts? Are there specific expectations or ranges of experience that might be involved within a context or among contexts? Theory devoid of practice can be lifeless, but if we work from experiences of learners and educators, we stand the possibility of finding new connections, meanings, and possibilities. Transformative learning has not been widely discussed in application to instructional practice other than to make suggestions. Building on research and generating new research from practice could powerfully accelerate our understanding.

And certainly we as educators have a responsibility to pursue the questions of ethics and responsibility where they relate to transformative learning. As we endeavor to introduce a dynamic strain of lifelong learning, how will it impact the life of the learner beyond the classroom? What are the responsibilities of educators and organizations to support learners through the dramatic changes of transformative learning? Where do we go to discuss these issues further? How can we move our understanding ahead in these areas? Self-assessment by educators does not stop in the first stage of this model; instead, it is grounded and permeated by reflective practice throughout. Asking difficult questions of ourselves about our purposes and responsibilities will bring us into better understanding the meanings and possibilities of transformative learning for teachers and learners.

CONCLUSION: A DYNAMIC MODEL OF TRANSFORMATIVE LEARNING IN OUR HANDS

Inherent in the model are generative, dynamic characteristics. Like transformative learning, this model is open-ended, includes continuing discovery, and fosters changing understandings. Never meant to confine anyone's goals and paths of learning, this model is a tool to help conceptualize, organize, and create learning opportunities that may lead to transformative learning. Its elements of lifelong learning skills and perspective enable a broad application across many contexts. The dynamic quality of the model supports and encourages teachers and learners alike to revise and reinterpret the model to benefit their instructional needs, goals, and possibilities.

The power of the Transformative Learning Opportunities Model rests in teachers and learners. Like transformative learning itself, the responsibility cannot be taken on by another. A framework is offered, the model laid forth, and imperatives for action delineated. The power of the process lies in our understanding of adult learning, our learners, their content, and context. The adult educator is the operative in moving the model from its potential into application. Developing transformative learning opportunities, facilitating exploration, and supporting inquiry are powerful roles that we can blend with learner responsibility. Learners can take such learning opportunities further, give them life, create their own constructions of how they understand and make meaning, and construct their futures. In so doing learners and educators bring transformative learning to life.

APPENDIX A

Diagrams of the Transformative Learning Opportunities Model

Developed from research of transformative learning experiences in several settings, this instructional design model offers guidelines for developing transformative learning opportunities (King, 1997, 2000, 2002, 2003a; King & Wright, 2003). Not a rigid formula, it is a series of considerations that one addresses in designing learning experiences for adults with transformative learning in mind. The model draws upon what we know about adult learners and the expectations they have for learning. It incorporates the findings of research across contexts and is built from how the learners experience transformative learning in diverse educational contexts. Rather than being a routine "recipe for success," it is a basis for developing open-ended, individualized, challenging, and stretching learning experiences for adult learners.

Chapter 2 discusses the model through details, graphics, and brief examples. The figures are duplicated in this appendix for easy reference. Figure 2.1 uses overlays, like transparencies, to emphasize that the work of the educator continues concurrently with the experience of the learners. These overlays enable us to visualize the co-existence and interdependence of these two pathways. Figures 2.2 and 2.3 portray the individual overlays, while Figure 2.4 again integrates the overlays and presents greater detail.

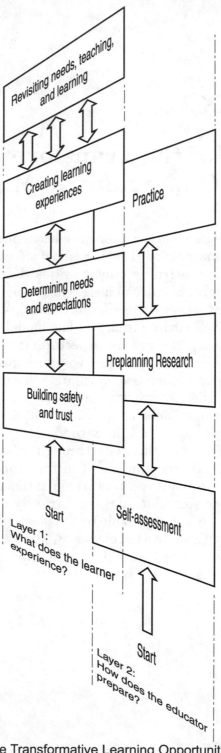

Figure 2.1 The Transformative Learning Opportunities Model.

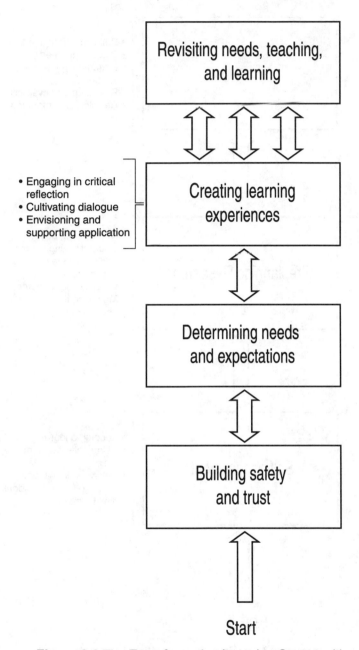

Figure 2.2 The Transformative Learning Opportunities Model, Layer 1:
What does the learner experience?

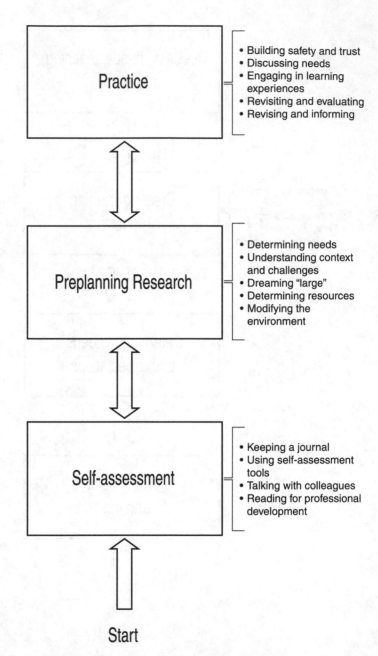

Figure 2.3 The Transformative Learning Opportunities Model, Layer 2:
How does the educator prepare?

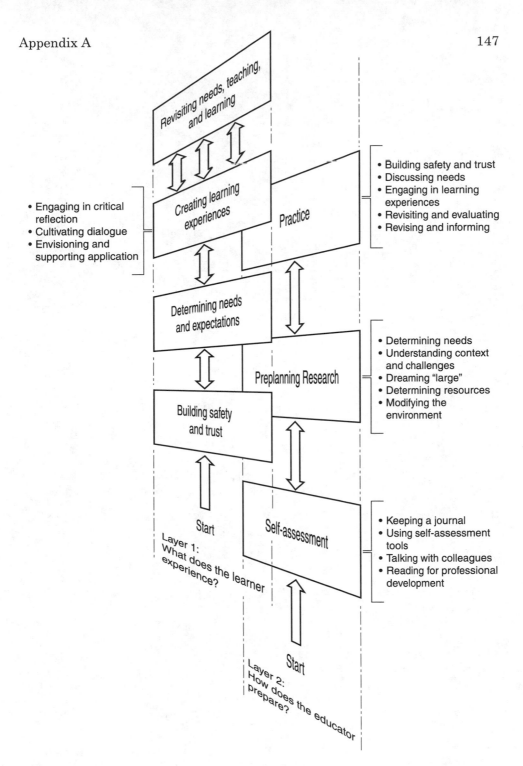

Figure 2.4 The Transformative Learning Opportunities Model in detail.

APPENDIX B

Materials for
Continuing Higher Education

INSTRUCTIONS: This appendix is a framework for planning, using the Transformative Learning Opportunities Model in Appendix A. We as educators will not need to answer all the questions here, but may use this to help us organize and develop unique, open-ended plans for our learners and context. Please refer to the section in Chapter 3, Continuing Higher Education, for instructions about how to use this material. The scenario is *Sociology 101: Diversity*.

EDUCATOR'S SELF-ASSESSMENT AND PREPLANNING

SELF-ASSESSMENT

- What are the objectives for this class?
- What are my goals for this class?
- What are my goals for these learners?
- What is my vision for these learners?
- What is my vision for myself as an educator?
- How might experiences of critical reflection and thinking impact these adults' learning, perspectives, and lives?
- What aspects of self-directed learning and lifelong learning could benefit them based on their goals and needs?
- How can I introduce these greater goals and benefits to these learners?
- How would transformative learning opportunities fit into this learning activity?
- What support can the organization and I offer these learners if they pursue transformative learning?

PREPLANNING RESEARCH

Determining Needs
- Who are these continuing higher education learners?
- What general needs do they have as a group?
- What do we know about their personal and professional goals?
- Are these new or continuing students?
- Are there any prerequisites to this course that would indicate their preparation or level of understanding?
- What other courses might they likely have taken?
- Are there any test results or other demonstration of proficiencies in this subject area by these learners?

Understanding Context and Challenges
- What is the mission of this institution?
- Does it serve a specific population of learners?
- What are the learners' and program's goals for the learners?
- How is success defined in this program?
- What is the expectation for evaluation of student performance?
- Are the learners from collectives, for example, a degree program or employer-sponsored program?
- What are the program's and the organization's climates regarding critical questioning and change?

Dreaming "Large"
- What preliminary objectives do the context and learners indicate at this point?
- Which of these objectives are required and which are optional?
- What other objectives might the learners have?
- What other objectives have learners in such classes had?

Determining Resources
- What resources will be available?
- Will we have a blackboard, whiteboard, flipchart, overhead projector, or LCD projector and computer to use?
- Is there a library or computer lab we can use to conduct research?
- Where and when will learners have access to libraries and computers?
- Is there a diversity policy for the institution and can it be distributed to the class?

- Is there a list of resources for additional reading and/or services on diversity issues and support that can be distributed?
- Are there specialists in the content area available to participate in the class?

Modifying the Environment
- Is the classroom furniture appropriate for adult use?
- Can the chairs be moved into groups?
- Are there tables available for group work?
- Can the environment include displays of multicultural appreciation (maps, posters, etc.)?

POTENTIAL OBSTACLES

What obstacles might I anticipate arising from the following and how can we overcome them?

	Obstacle	Solution
Organizational environment and program		
Degree requirements		
Schedule or time constraints		
Diverse cultures		
Communication problems		
Personality styles		
Learning styles		
Teaching and learning orientation (traditional vs. student-centered)		
Student course load for the semester		

STRATEGIES

Review Appendix G for a complete list of instructional strategies that might apply to this setting. What teaching and learning strategies have been especially successful for me?
- With these continuing higher education learners.
- With continuing higher education learners in general.
- With this learning activity.
- With this general content area.

LEARNING ACTIVITY PLAN
Sociology 101: Diversity

1. Introduction and welcome
   a. Initiate group discussion. What different subgroups do you iden-
      tify with (family, ethnic, class, gender, occupation, etc.)? What
      generalizations do people make about your group? How can gen-
      eralizations harm individuals and groups? What positive pur-
      poses can generalizations serve?
   b. Give brief introduction to the unit and relevant terms, including
      people groups, socialization, acculturation, integration, individu-
      ation, social alienation, cultural history, and social history.

2. Students' needs and expectations
   a. Initiate class discussion. Post responses on flipchart, blackboard,
      or whiteboard.
      • Which of these terms are familiar and which are not?
      • What other terms and issues do they want to explore?
      • Where have they seen these topics or issues arise in their per-
        sonal and professional lives?
      • How could they use the learning from this learning activity in
        their professional and personal lives?
      • What will they set as their goals for this session?
   b. Provide validation of their goals.
   c. Incorporate as many of their goals as possible in this learning
      activity.
   d. Communicate which goals will be included in this learning activ-
      ity and which will hopefully be addressed in future classes.

3. Presentation of sample strategies to use in this assignment. The class
   discusses and chooses one or more.
   a. Small group discussions
   b. Case study
   c. Role-playing
   d. Group presentations
   e. Journaling
   f. Dramatic scene or reading
4. Facilitating the learning activities. This sample learning activity has
   the students selecting case study and small group work activities.
   a. Explain case study group discussion process. Answer questions.

b. Group prereads the case study.
c. Use this excerpt from Chapter 3 as an example:

   . . . Martin [the professor] *starts the discussion session with a series of open-ended questions about the group process and how people may have varied perspectives based on their personal and cultural histories. Using an example from his own experience, he reveals how his cultural background had obscured his understanding of some ethnic groups in the past. He then refers to the discussion questions and asks the class how they used the first case, about a gay couple moving into a working-class family neighborhood, to help understand not only themselves, but also others.*

d. Still assembled in the larger group, students develop preliminary questions, such as:
   - What would be my initial reaction to the situation?
   - Why would I react that way?
   - What would be my unspoken and spoken comments to my neighbors and to the couple?
   - Would I have fears or hesitation?
   - Where could such feelings come from (culture, family, friends, etc.)?
   - In what sense am I part of a minority group (religion, race, class, family history, etc.)?
   - How do I feel when I am treated differently or unjustly?
   - How can I look beyond my preconceived expectations and stereotypes to act differently?
   - How have I responded to people different from myself in my neighborhood or at work?
   - What conflicts or difficulties have I seen or would I expect?

e. Give final instructions for the small group process, including the three guidelines:
   (1) Have respect for other opinions.
   (2) Allow equal time for members to speak.
   (3) Collectively question reasons for views and decisions.
f. Clarify the professor's role as facilitator and students' roles as collaborators.
g. Visit the small groups, providing limited input.
   - Encourage the students to ask deeper questions of differences and meaning.
   - When difficulties are identified, reflect them to the group to consider the circumstances and issues.

         ·   Encourage support and respect.

         ·   Emphasize the negotiation of differences.

         ·   Recommend where resources might be accessed.

  h. Observe and evaluate these key progress points.

         ·   Introduction and prereading

         ·   Group development of questions

         ·   Group understanding of the content

         ·   Group dialogue and dynamics

5. Conclusion. Use small group presentations as a synthesizing activity.

  a. Facilitate group presentations, using the following questions as guides.

         ·   What difficulties had they envisioned for this case?

         ·   What examples did they have from their own lives?

         ·   How did they respond?

         ·   What did they conclude?

         ·   What further questions did they pursue?

         ·   What questions are still unanswered?

6. Evaluation and follow-up

  a. Complete the student evaluations through observations of small groups and presentations.

    i. Learning related to transformative learning

         ·   What did they learn about themselves in relationship to the case?

         ·   What did they learn about themselves through the group experience?

         ·   What personal or social assumptions did they reveal?

         ·   How can they learn to question new ideas, information, and controversies as self-directed adult learners?

         ·   Did they critically question generalizations and stereotypes? And if so, how did they?

         ·   How did they communicate respect for views different from their own?

         ·   How did they articulate issues and conflicts with different people groups?

    ii. Content learning gains

         ·   Related sociology terms and concepts

         ·   Application of sociological concepts to real situations

     •   Broader implications of their learning
     •   Exploration of deeper issues involved in social interactions

  b. Complete the professor evaluation using your reflective journal, student feedback about facilitation needs and group process, and student evaluation forms.

7. Extension. Consider additional possibilities that students and professor may pursue.
  a. Present role-playing scenarios as developed by each small group.
  b. Invite a guest panel to discuss different experiences as minorities in society.
  c. Conduct field research by observing and interviewing members of different communities.
  d. Create critical incidents to be used with sociology learners.
  e. Select the next case materials based on interests and needs that surfaced in this learning activity.

8. Recommendations for further revisions
  a. Consider where problems arose and how to prevent them.
  b. Review the questions the students had and improve ways to clarify the assignment from the beginning.
  c. Consider how additional guidance may be suggested for personally and collectively dealing with diversity issues.
  d. Consider how students may maximize self-directed learning skills in this assignment.
  e. Consider alternative extension assignments as suggested or needed.

APPENDIX C

Materials for Adult English Speakers of Other Languages (ESOL)

INSTRUCTIONS: This appendix is a framework for planning, using the Transformative Learning Opportunities Model in Appendix A. We as educators will not need to answer all the questions here, but may use this to help us organize and develop unique, open-ended plans for our learners and context. Please refer to the section in Chapter 3, Adult English Speakers of Other Languages (ESOL), for instructions about how to use this material. The scenario is *Reading American Literature: Revealing New Perspectives and Questions.*

EDUCATOR'S SELF-ASSESSMENT AND PREPLANNING

SELF-ASSESSMENT

- What are the objectives for this ESOL class?
- What are my goals for this ESOL class?
- What are my goals for these learners?
- What is my vision for these learners?
- What is my vision for myself as an educator?
- How might experiences of critical reflection and thinking impact these learners' learning, perspectives, and lives?
- What aspects of self-directed learning and lifelong learning could benefit them based on their goals and needs?
- How can I introduce these greater goals and benefits to these learners?
- How could transformative learning opportunities benefit these learners and fit into this learning activity?
- What support can the organization and I offer these learners if they pursue transformative learning?

PREPLANNING RESEARCH

Determining Needs
*   Who are these ESOL learners?
*   What ESOL needs do they have?
*   How many have a secondary school diploma or college degree?
*   What other ESOL courses have they taken?
*   What do we know about their personal and professional goals?
*   Are there any test results or other demonstration of proficiencies in English language learning available for these learners?

Understanding Context and Challenges
*   What is the mission of this organization and program?
*   What are the organization's and the program's goals for these learners?
*   Are these learners from a collective, for example, a degree program, or place of employment?
*   How is success defined in this organization and program?
*   How will the organization and the program expect learners to be evaluated?
*   What is the climate of the organization and the program regarding change and questioning the status quo?

Dreaming "Large"
*   What preliminary objectives do the context and learners indicate at this point?
*   Which of these objectives are required and which are optional?
*   What other objectives might the learners have?
*   Are the ESOL learners expected to reach a specific proficiency or test score at the end of this class?
*   What other objectives have learners in such classes had?

Determining Resources
*   What resources will be available?
*   Will the students buy books or other reading materials or does the program supply them?
*   Will we have a blackboard, whiteboard, flipchart, overhead projector, or LCD projector and computer to use?
*   Is there a library or computer lab we can use to conduct research?
*   Where and when will learners have access to libraries and computers?

Modifying the Environment
*   Is the environment accessible to ESOL learners? If not, what can be

done about it?
- Is there sufficient and prepared staff to guide learners in finding the classrooms and any materials they need to bring?
- Is the classroom furniture appropriate for adult use?
- Can the environment include displays of international and multi-cultural appreciation, maps, posters, etc?
- Is the environment free of ethnocentric and childish displays?
- Is the environment free from distractions?

POTENTIAL OBSTACLES

What obstacles might I anticipate arising from the following and how can we overcome them?

	Obstacle	Solution
Environment and program		
Schedule or time constraints		
Holidays or vacation conflicts		
Diverse cultures		
Communication problems		
Weather/climate		
Cultural preferences		
Personality styles		
Learning styles		
Teaching and learning orientation (traditional vs. student-centered)		
Educational background		
ESOL challenges (vocabulary, comprehension, etc.)		

STRATEGIES

Review Appendix G for a complete list of instructional strategies that might apply to this setting. What teaching and learning strategies have been especially successful for me?
- With these ESOL learners.
- With ESOL learners in general.

- With this learning activity.
- With this general content area.

LEARNING ACTIVITY PLAN
Reading American Literature:
Revealing New Perspectives and Questions

1. Introduction and welcome
    a. Have an icebreaker. Define *urban* and *rural* and discuss with the class some examples of each. Learners take these three questions and briefly interview three classmates.
        - What country did you primarily live in as a youngster and young adult?
        - Did you live in an urban or rural setting?
        - Could you briefly describe the setting?
    b. Initiate group discussion.
        - How many were brought up in rural settings?
        - How many in urban settings?
        - What crops did they raise in rural settings in their countries of origin?
    c. Welcome the learners. Emphasize the diversity and richness of their experiences. Articulate the breadth of knowledge contained in learning the language of a host culture. Through their readings in this class they will be exploring not only the language but also U.S. culture and history.

2. Learners' needs and expectations
    a. Initiate class discussion. Post responses on flipchart, blackboard, or whiteboard.
        - Why are you learning English?
        - What are your goals for taking this specific class?
        - How does this unit of study fit in with these goals?
        - What do you need to learn about English (vocabulary, reading, writing, etc.)?
        - For what specific settings or areas do you need to learn English (e.g. school, work, medical needs, etc.)?
    b. Provide validation of their goals. Indicate if and where certain goals will be met in other courses (advanced topics).
    c. Incorporate as many of their goals as possible in this learning activity.

    d. Communicate which goals will be included in this learning activity and which will hopefully be addressed in future classes.

3. Presentation of sample strategies to use in this assignment. The class discusses and chooses one or more.
    a. Small group discussions
    b. Research inquiry about the story's setting (e.g., social, cultural, political, or economic)
    c. Group presentations
    d. Collaborative writing
    e. Journaling
    f. Dramatic scene or reading

4. Facilitating the learning activities. This sample learning activity has the learners selecting small group work and presentations as activities.
    a. Excerpt from Chapter 3:

Earlier in the course, the students selected three short stories from an annotated list of 15. They have selected one each for a historical piece, contemporary author, and a racial perspective. After choosing the reading material, the group then discusses the issues they will address with each of them. The primary focus of the class is language learning. Written and oral progress are both the goals. At the same time, students can also use this opportunity to learn more about the American/host culture and are encouraged to develop questions that reach beyond the story's surface into the lives, beliefs, values, and cultures of the characters.

    b. With the large group, present and clarify these critical questions. Then the learners assemble in small groups to review the story and discuss the questions.
- What is different about the lives of the characters in this reading?
- What are the expectations of the characters? And how are they different from today? Or from your own experiences?
- Describe the environment of the characters. How is it different from today? Or from your past experience?
- Why are there such differences?
- How do the differences affect them as individuals and as communities?
- What issues may be behind these differences?
- Are there other questions you would like to discuss?

   c.   Excerpt from Chapter 3:
        At this point, the learners have read the historical short story
        study. In their respective groups they discuss what the text and
        their research reveal about the specific time period. Some stu-
        dents see the historical setting very differently from others and
        the dialogue is about the similarities and differences of their ob-
        servations.
   d.   Clarify the role of facilitator and the students' roles as co-learners.
   e.   Visit the small groups, providing limited input.
        ·   Encourage the learners to ask deeper questions of differ-
            ences and meaning.
        ·   Encourage the learners to use their experience, understand-
            ing, and research to resolve differences and find answers.
        ·   Recommend where resources might be accessed.
   f.   Observe and evaluate these key progress points.
        ·   Discussion of questions
        ·   Conducting research
        ·   Recording responses
        ·   In-depth discussions
        ·   Sharing of experiences

5. Conclusion. Use group presentations as a synthesizing activity.
   a.   Listen to small group presentations, which include:
        ·   Their conclusions
        ·   Issues about the story and the countries within which they
            were raised
        ·   Time to answer questions from the other groups
   b.   Facilitate a class synthesis of all of the small group presentations.
        ·   Why are there such differences?
        ·   How do the differences affect learners as individuals and as
            communities?
        ·   What issues may be behind these differences?
        ·   What could make a difference in these disparities?

6. Evaluation and follow-up
   a.   Complete the student evaluations through observations of small
        groups and presentations.
        i.   Learning related to transformative learning
             ·   Within this context, these learners may find themselves
                 questioning and analyzing their native culture and lan-
                 guage, their preconceptions of the English language and

U.S. culture, and their self-understanding.
- How do they articulate these issues and conflicts with the host language?
- How do they learn through others' questions?
- How can they help one another see different perspectives?
- Have they, and if so how, used different avenues of expression to create their understanding of the culture and issues? (Perhaps through shared history, culture, rituals, or music.)
- How can they continue to question new ideas, information, and controversies as self-directed adult learners?
- Did they, and if so how, critically question, analyze information, seek out resources, and/or synthesize their views and understanding?

ii. Content learning gains
- Vocabulary
- History and culture
- Group communications skills
- Communication of abstract concepts
- Critical thinking skills

b. Complete the teacher evaluation using your reflective journal and student feedback about facilitation needs.

7. Extension. Consider additional possibilities that learners and teacher may pursue.
   a. Write individual or collaborative integrative essays.
   b. View a movie or documentary regarding U.S. rural life then and now.
   c. Select the next reading material based on interest and needs that surfaced in this learning activity.

8. Recommendations for further revisions
   a. Consider where problems arose and how to prevent them.
   b. Review the questions the students had and improve ways to clarify the assignment from the beginning.
   c. Consider providing access to resources that are difficult for the students to get.
   d. Consider how students may maximize self-directed learning skills in this assignment.
   e. Review specific difficulties in communication skills.

APPENDIX D

Materials for
Adult Basic Education (ABE)

INSTRUCTIONS: This appendix is a framework for planning, using the Transformative Learning Opportunities Model in Appendix A. We as educators will not need to answer all the questions here, but may use this to help us organize and develop unique, open-ended plans for our learners and context. Please refer to the section in Chapter 3, Adult Basic Education (ABE) for instructions about how to use this material. The scenario is *Renovation Project: Integrated Basic Skills*.

EDUCATOR'S SELF- ASSESSMENT AND PREPLANNING

SELF-ASSESSMENT

- What are the objectives for this ABE class?
- What are my goals for this class?
- What are my goals for these learners?
- What is my vision for these learners, immediately and in the distant future?
- What is my vision for myself as an educator working with these learners?
- How might experiences of critical reflection and thinking impact these adults' learning, perspectives, and futures?
- What aspects of self-directed and lifelong learning could benefit them based on their goals and needs?
- How does creating transformative learning opportunities expand this learning activity's impact?
- How can I introduce these greater goals and benefits to these students?
- What support can the organization and I offer these learners if they pursue transformative learning?

PREPLANNING RESEARCH

Determining Needs
- Who are these learners?
- What needs do they have?
- What other courses have they taken?
- What do we know about their personal and professional goals? Are there any test results or other demonstration of proficiencies (e.g., TABE, B*EST, GED) by these learners?

Understanding Context and Challenges
- What is the mission of this program and organization? What are the organization's or the program's goals for these learners?
- How is success defined in this organization or program?
- What are the specifications for students' learning evaluation?

Dreaming "Large"
- What preliminary objectives would the context and learners indicate at this point?
- Which of these objectives are required and which are optional?
- What other objectives might the learners have?
- What other objectives have learners in such classes had?

Determining Resources
- What resources will be available?
- Will the students buy books or other materials or does the program supply them?
- Will we have a blackboard, whiteboard, flipchart, overhead projector, or LCD projector and computer to use?
- Is there a library or computer lab we can use to conduct research?
- Where and when will learners have access to libraries and computers?
- Can they visit a renovation site and a building supply warehouse?
- Do we have adequate copies of the blueprints and catalogs they will need?

Modifying the Environment
- Is the classroom furniture appropriate for adult use?
- Do we have adequate table space to lay out the materials learners will be using?
- Is the room large enough so groups will not be crowded together?

POTENTIAL OBSTACLES

What obstacles might I anticipate arising from the following and how can we overcome them?

	Obstacle	Solution
Environment and program		
Schedule or time constraints		
Negative prior educational experiences		
Different educational and professional goals		
Differences in student motivation		
Collaboration skills		
Different cultural preferences		
Personality styles		
Learning styles		
Teaching and learning orientation (traditional vs. student-centered)		
ABE challenges (vocabulary, critical thinking, abstract thinking, etc.)		

STRATEGIES

Review Appendix G for a complete list of instructional strategies that might apply to this setting. What teaching and learning strategies have been especially successful for me?
- With these ABE learners.
- With ABE learners in general.
- With this learning activity.
- With this general content area.

LEARNING ACTIVITY PLAN
Renovation Project: Integrated Basic Skills

Excerpt from Chapter 3:
These learners funnel into the classroom and go to their bookcases to retrieve their materials. They then gather in groups around tables to work

on the project in progress. They spread floor plans, materials lists, and catalogs across the tables. The students have been assigned to work as teams and renovate a small warehouse into living quarters. While they begin with a sound structure with heating, cooling, and plumbing systems, they have to design a floor plan, divide up the floor space, and order materials for walls, flooring, electrical, plumbing, heating, and cooling. It is a mammoth task, but as a whole the class faces it with determination and excitement.

The learners had started off with a class discussion of possible projects they could work on and chose this one because the neighborhood has a few unused warehouses and a community organization is considering renovating one as a contractor's speculation model. The work they do on this project can help give the organization some ideas of possible layouts, costs, and time commitments. This classroom assignment is an opportunity to take a real-life problem and build real solutions.

1. Introduction and learners' needs and expectations
   a. Present topic and facilitate group decisions. Several possible construction projects are provided to the learners.
      • The class discusses each project and decides on the one which they will undertake.
      • The learners self-select groups.
      • Groups separately develop and plan for the same project.
      • Groups decide if they will only have internal evaluation or invite external evaluation of their final projects.
      • Groups decide on assignments to be included in the project (essays, journals, presentations, etc.).
   b. Discuss goals.
      • What might they learn about in this project?
      • Who has experience in construction, home repair, or improvement?
      • What ABE skills will they be able to use and learn?
      • What benefits could this type of project have?
      • How might their work be used outside of the classroom?
      • What individual goals will they set for this project?
   c. Provide validation of their goals. Indicate where certain goals will be met in other courses (e.g., advanced topics).
   d. Incorporate as many of their goals as possible in this learning activity.

    e. Communicate which goals will be included in this learning activity and which will hopefully be addressed in future classes.

2. Presentation of sample strategies to use in this assignment. Class discusses and chooses one or more.
    a. Project based learning
    b. Case study
    c. Small group discussions
    d. Research
    e. Group presentations
    f. Collaborative learning
    g. Group dynamics
    h. Journaling

3. Facilitating the learning activities. This sample learning activity has the students selecting case study and small group work as activities.
    a. With the large group, present and clarify these initial planning questions.
       · What will be involved in this project?
       · How will the students divide the labor?
       · How will they find information they need?
       · What questions will they ask on their site visits?
       · What experts might they consult?
       · How will they overcome obstacles?
       · How do they feel about undertaking this project?
       · What opportunities might this experience bring with it?
       · What other questions they would like to discuss?
    b. Clarify instructor's role as facilitator and students' roles as members of the project team.
    c. Visit the small groups, providing limited input.
       · Encourage the students to use their experience, understanding, and research to find answers and make decisions.
       · Encourage the students to ask deeper questions of differences in expectations or opinions.
       · Emphasize the negotiation of differences.
       · Recommend where resources might be accessed including computer-based information, catalogs, and floor plans.
       · Conduct at least one troubleshooting session each week with each group.
    d. Observe and evaluate these key progress points.

- Project choice and evaluation decisions
- Group dynamics
- Division of labor
- Research effectiveness
- Daily and weekly reports
- Weekly troubleshooting sessions
- In-depth discussions

4. Conclusion
   a. Facilitate group presentations. Use group presentations as a synthesizing activity.
      - Present their completed project.
      - Discuss their group process. What did they do to create their solution?
      - Identify learning the students gained in professional skills and ABE learning.
      - Present any unresolved questions.
      - Answer questions from the other groups.
   b. Facilitate a class synthesis of all of the small group experiences in this project. (See evaluation next section.)

5. Evaluation and follow-up
   a. Complete the student evaluations through observations of small groups and presentations.
      i. Learning related to transformative learning. Conduct debriefing of each group with the following or other questions.
         - Did they, and if so how, work through the tasks and related problems the same way individually?
         - How did they work through problems and challenges as a group?
         - How did they critically question, analyze information, seek out resources, and/or make decisions together?
         - Did they find that sometimes information was not consistent? If so, how did they deal with it?
         - How can they continue to question new or conflicting information as self-directed adult learners?
         - Do they feel more confident about their ability to pursue such a complex project?
         - What does that mean for them as adults and as adult learners?
         - How are they going to apply the specific knowledge and

the broader lessons they were learning in their testing experience and their personal and professional lives?
- Did their learning, abilities, or point of view look different to them now? And if so in what ways? And to what degree lesser or greater?

ii. Content learning gains
- Vocabulary, math, reading, and research skills
- Group communications skills
- Critical thinking skills
- Problem solving skills
- Decision making skills

iii. Project learning
- Evaluation by peers
- Evaluation by instructor
- Evaluation by outside expert (if this has been chosen by learners)

b. Complete the instructor evaluation using your reflective journal, student feedback about facilitation needs and group process, and student evaluation forms.

6. Extension. Consider additional possibilities that students and instructor may pursue.
a. Assign individual or collaborative integrative essays.
b. Select instructional strategies and projects based on interest in and success of the current project.
c. Select future projects based on needs that surfaced in this learning activity.
d. Pursue learning opportunities to employ critical thinking in continued research.
e. Suggest enrollment in comparative literature courses.
f. Suggest study of urban renewal initiatives.
g. Pursue study of critical thinking and research skills as consumers.
h. Build a resource list for continued learning in ABE skills, construction skills, common construction regulations and codes, urban renewal, critical thinking, or computer-aided design.

7. Recommendations for further revisions
a. Consider where problems arose and how to prevent them.
b. Consider what was learned from problems that were encountered.
c. Review questions the students had and improve ways to clarify

the assignment from the beginning.

d. Consider providing access to resources that are difficult for the students to get.

e. Consider how students may maximize self-directed learning skills in this assignment.

f. Consider providing an outside resource person for consultation for each team.

g. Evaluate benefits and drawbacks of the site visits.

APPENDIX E

Materials for Workplace Learning

INSTRUCTIONS: This appendix is a framework for planning, using the Transformative Learning Opportunities Model in Appendix A. We as educators will not need to answer all the questions here, but may use this to help us organize and develop unique, open-ended plans for our learners and context. Please refer to the section in Chapter 3, Workplace Learning, for instructions about how to use this material. The scenario is *Sanking Financial: Technology Learning and Customer Service.*

TRAINER'S SELF- ASSESSMENT AND PREPLANNING

SELF-ASSESSMENT

- What are the objectives for this training class?
- What are my goals for this class?
- What are my goals for these learners?
- What is my vision for what these learners will be able to understand and do?
- What is my vision for myself as an educator?
- How might experiences of critical reflection and thinking impact these learners' learning, perspectives, and work?
- What aspects of self-directed and lifelong learning could benefit them based on their goals and needs?
- How can I introduce these greater goals and benefits to these learners?
- How can transformative learning opportunities benefit the learners and the organization?
- What support can the organization and I offer these learners if they pursue transformative learning?

PREPLANNING RESEARCH

Determining General Needs
- Who are these learners?
- What individual and collective needs do they have?
- How many have a secondary school diploma or college degree?
- What other training sessions have they taken?
- What do we know about their personal and professional goals?
- Are there any test results or demonstration of proficiencies in the area of focus?

Understanding Context and Challenges
- What is the mission and vision of this organization?
- What is the mission and vision of this training initiative?
- What are the organization's or program's goals for this training initiative? For these learners?
- How is success defined in this organization or program?
- Will the learners be evaluated? And if so, how?

Dreaming "Large"
- What preliminary objectives do the context and learners indicate at this point?
- Which of these objectives are required and which are optional?
- What other objectives might the learners have?
- What other objectives have learners in such classes had?

Determining Resources
- What resources will be available?
- Will we have a blackboard, whiteboard, flipchart, overhead projector, or LCD projector and computer to use?
- Will the learners have the reading material beforehand?
- Will all participants receive copies of the software tutorial and accompanying materials?
- Will all learners be able to access email and web bulletin board days before the session?
- What additional research resources will be available?

Modifying the Environment
- Is there sufficient room for learners to spread out their materials?

- Are the power and network ports easily accessible and working?
- Is there adequate ventilation in the room where the computers will be used?
- Can the area be made free of distractions and interruptions?

POTENTIAL OBSTACLES

What obstacles might I anticipate arising from the following and how can we overcome them?

	Obstacle	Solution
Environment and program		
Schedule or time constraints		
Competing responsibilities		
Organizational expectations		
Learner expectations		
Diverse cultures		
Communication problems		
Personality styles		
Learning styles		
Teaching and learning orientation (traditional vs. student-centered)		
Educational background		
Technical expertise challenges		
Technical difficulties		
Technical support		

STRATEGIES

Review Appendix G for a complete list of instructional strategies that might apply to this setting. What teaching and learning strategies have been especially successful for me?
- With these learners.
- With this company's culture.
- With workplace learners in general.

- With this learning activity.
- With this general content area.

LEARNING ACTIVITY PLAN
Sanking Financial: Technology Learning and
Customer Service

1. Introduction and welcome
   a. Begin icebreaker. Write down answers to two of the following ques-
       tions on separate index cards.
       - What is my favorite computer program?
       - What is my most common frustration with computers?
       - What was my most amusing customer service problem?
       Hand in the cards and then have them redistributed. Next people
       try to match them up with their owners.
   b. Welcome the learners. Emphasize the breadth and similarities of
       their work experiences. Articulate the breadth of knowledge they
       have of the field.
   Discuss the following questions.
       - How many computer programs do they use per day?
       - How many applications and customers do they deal with each
         week?
       - How many problems do they solve daily?
   Emphasize that the participants are experts. The session is aimed to
   build on this success and help them advance further.

2. Learners' needs and expectations
   a. Initiate class discussion. Post responses on a flipchart or LCD
       screen.
       - What do you want to learn in these sessions?
       - What are your expectations?
       - What are your goals for taking this class?
       - What do you need to learn about this computer program?
       - What customer service challenges do you face?
   b. Provide validation of their goals. Indicate where certain goals will
       be met in other courses (e.g., advanced topics).
   c. Incorporate as many of their goals as possible in this class.
   d. Communicate which goals will be included in this class.
   e. Offer to communicate the other goals to the organization if they
       would like.

3. Presentation of sample strategies to use in this assignment. The class
discusses and chooses one or more.
    a. Small group discussions
    b. Self-evaluations
    c. Online discussion boards
    d. Question and answer sessions
    e. Short case scenarios
    f. Problem-based learning
    g. Software demonstration and interactive presentation
    h. Learner-developed case book
    i. Learner-developed frequently asked questions (FAQs)
    j. Group presentations
    k. Collaborative writing
    l. Journaling

4. Facilitating the learning activities. This sample learning activity has
    the learners selecting critical questioning, interactive demonstration,
    and small group work as activities.
    a. Pose and clarify a selection of these initial critical questions.
        •   What do they want to learn about the software?
        •   What problems with the software do they anticipate?
        •   What are common software problems they have had in the
            past with applications?
        •   What customer service problems do they encounter related to
            applications?
        •   What were some of the needs their customers had in these
            regards?
        •   How did they meet their customers' needs?
        •   What were other common short-term and long-term needs of
            which applicants might not have been aware?
        •   How might the customer be looking at situations in a differ-
            ent way based on their geographical and cultural context, their
            occupation, their socio-economic status, or their extenuating
            circumstances?
        •   What other questions would they like to discuss?
    b. Clarify their relationship as co-learners.
    c. Introduce the "What-if" question and answer format .
        Excerpt from Chapter 3:
            Gradually the discussion moves into the new format of "What-
            if" and Frank [the trainer] *poses several scenarios of difficulties*

they might encounter with applicants. Several complex scenarios are posed and rapid-fire responses are expected. The learners are getting used to this format now and provide many responses to each case. Then Frank quickly moves to the next scenario. After a series of these interactions, he suddenly stops and says, "Where are the problems?" and this is the cue for the loan officers to dig deeper into the situations of the customers and consider the difficult questions, issues, and concerns they might have. This discussion is preparatory for the extended case they will consider later, but at this early point in the session they already uncover complexities and issues that oftentimes lie beneath the surface unaddressed.

d. Present an interactive demonstration that includes:
  - Provide an orientation to software and basic functions.
  - Input a sample client loan application.
  - Run loan application through for approval.
  - Follow program comments.
  - Provide overview of Help screens.
  - Demonstrate how to share files and functions.
  - Introduce functions to perform overrides for exceptions, access screens, and functions.
  - Demonstrate additional stipulations screens and functions.

e. Visit the small groups, providing limited input.
  - Encourage the learners to ask deeper questions of differences and meaning.
  - Encourage learners to discuss relevant difficult customer service experiences they have had in the past and explore possible or additional solutions.
  - Encourage the learners to use their experience, understanding and research to resolve differences and find answers.
  - Recommend they build a list of questions that remain unresolved.

f. Observe and evaluate these key progress points.
  - Online discussion prior to class session
  - Discussion of needs and expectations
  - Interest and dialogue about critical questions
  - "What-if" dynamics, successes, and problems
  - Interactive presentation dynamics, successes, and problems
  - Case scenario study
  - Small group discussions dynamics, successes, and problems

- Follow-up discussions in class and online

5. Conclusion. Use small group presentations as a synthesizing activity.
   a. Facilitate small group presentations, using the following questions as guides.
      - What problems were identified?
      - What underlying issues were evident?
      - What additional problems could there be?
      - How can they solve problems?
      - What do they need to watch out for?
      - What solutions were suggested?
      - Did they build collaborative solutions?
      - Did they gain any different perspectives?
      - Are there unresolved questions and issues?
   b. Guide follow-up discussions on these possible topics.
      - Share their conclusions and suggestions.
      - Discuss dilemmas encountered.
      - Explore unresolved issues.
      - Consider additional learning they may have gained.
   c. Facilitate a class discussion that synthesizes all of the small group presentations, asking, what different prior experiences were helpful to explore and understand?

6. Evaluation and Follow-up
   a. Complete the learner evaluations through observations of small groups and online discussions.
      i. Learning related to transformative learning
         - How did they identify unspoken needs of applicants?
         - What did they find the easiest and hardest needs to identify?
         - How might their customers look at situations in very different ways based on their geographical and cultural context, their occupation, their socioeconomic status, or their extenuating circumstances?
         - How did they fare with the learner-centered format? Why was it difficult or comfortable?
         - What problem-solving and learning strategies did they learn?
         - How could critical questioning be helpful in their decision-making?
         - How can they practice questioning new ideas, informa-

tion, and controversies as self-directed adult learners?
- Did they critically question, analyze information, seek out resources, and/or synthesize their views and understanding? Which was the hardest part for them?
- What will they do with their new ideas about learning?

ii. Content learning gains
- Software skills
- Customer service proficiency
- Communications skills
- Problem solving skills. For example, how could the loan officer gather additional information? What alternative solutions were available?
- Critical thinking skills. For example, what additional needs might applicants need to consider that they might not be aware of? What problems might be embedded in a given application? Were there additional possibilities that might be relevant in this situation?

   b. Complete the trainer evaluation using your reflective journal and student feedback about instructional strategies.

7. Extension. Consider additional possibilities that learners and trainer may pursue.
   a. Present role-playing scenarios as developed by each group.
   b. Select the next case materials based on the interest generated in this one.
   c. Select future materials based on the needs that surfaced in this learning activity.
   d. Emphasize learner-developed frequently asked questions (FAQs) for the software and customer service guidelines. These can be posted on their company server.
   e. Continue online discussion of cases weekly.

8. Recommendations for further revisions.
   a. Consider where problems arose and how to prevent them.
   b. Review questions the learners had and how to clarify assignments.
   c. Refine existing cases and create additional ones to address the issues learners identified.
   d. Consider how learners may maximize self-directed learning skills in this assignment.

APPENDIX F

Materials for Faculty Development

INSTRUCTIONS: This appendix is a framework for planning, using the Transformative Learning Opportunities Model in Appendix A. We as educators will not need to answer all the questions here, but may use this to help organize and develop unique, open-ended plans for our learners and context. Please refer to the section in Chapter 3, Faculty Development, for instructions about how to use this material. The scenario is *Learner-Centered Classrooms: Collaborative Curriculum Development.*

DEVELOPER'S SELF- ASSESSMENT AND PREPLANNING

SELF-ASSESSMENT

- What are the objectives for this professional development session? For the larger professional development program?
- What are my goals for this session? For these learners?
- What is my vision for these learners in the immediate and distant future?
- What is my vision for myself as a developer? As a developer with this specific group of faculty?
- What aspects of self-directed learning and lifelong learning could benefit them based on their goals and needs?
- How can I introduce these greater goals and benefits to these learners?
- How can developers serve as resources to cultivate self-directed lifelong learning perspectives and strategies?
- How can developers serve as facilitators in faculty determining additional individual and collective needs?
- What benefits would transformative learning opportunities have for these faculty within the context of this session, program, and their work?

- What support can the organization and I offer these learners if they pursue transformative learning?

PREPLANNING RESEARCH

Determining Needs
- Who are these faculty learners?
- What professional development needs do they have?
- Within which other professional development classes or courses have they participated?
- What do we know about their personal and professional goals?
- Is there any level of proficiency or prior session required for entry into this session?

Understanding Context and Challenges
- What is the mission and vision of this institution?
- What is the mission and vision of the faculty's academic program?
- What are the program's goals for the student learners?
- What additional demands do the faculty have on them? Do these demands complement or conflict with the development sessions?
- How is success defined in this program and institution, both for the faculty member and for the program?

Dreaming "Large"
- What preliminary objectives do the context and learners indicate at this point?
- Which of these objectives are required and which are optional?
- What other objectives might these faculty learners have?
- What other objectives have faculty learners in such classes had?

Determining Resources
- What resources will be available?
- Will materials need to be purchased or copies made?
- Will we have a blackboard, whiteboard, flipchart, overhead projector, or LCD projector and computer to use?
- Where and when will these faculty have access to additional resources and/or computers?
- What amount of time is available in which to accommodate these sessions and outside work?

Modifying the Environment
- Is the classroom furniture appropriate for adult use?
- Can the chairs be moved into groups?
- Are there tables available for the faculty to be able to spread out their materials?
- Will the faculty be free from distraction and disturbance by other personnel and office demands during the session?
- If computers will be used, is there adequate ventilation in the room?

POTENTIAL OBSTACLES

What obstacles might I anticipate arising from the following and how can we overcome them?

	Obstacle	Solution
Environment and program		
Schedule or time constraints		
Interruptions		
Learner expectations		
Different technical computer expertise levels		
Prior negative experiences with professional development		
Conflicting professional needs or goals		
Communication problems		
Personality styles		
Learning styles		
Teaching and learning orientation (traditional vs. student-centered)		
Background in instructional strategies		
Program cultural climate		

STRATEGIES

Review Appendix G for a complete list of instructional strategies that might apply to this setting.

What teaching and learning strategies have been especially successful
for me?
- With these faculty learners.
- With faculty learners in general.
- With this learning activity.
- With this general content area.

LEARNING ACTIVITY ACTION PLAN
Learner-Centered Classrooms:
Collaborative Curriculum Development

1. Introduction and welcome
   a. Initiate group discussion.
      - What professional needs do the faculty recognize?
      - How can these different needs be met in an integrated and
        extended project?
      - What is their availability and time frame?
      - What constraints do they have upon them?
      - What formats do they want to use?
   b. Present a welcome to the faculty.
      - Emphasize the depth and richness of their expertise and ex-
        perience as educators.
      - Articulate the significant challenge they face in addressing
        their teaching and learning orientations and the resources
        they will have.
      - Encourage them with some possibilities of the benefits of their
        work in this project.

2. Faculty's needs and expectations
   a. Initiate class discussion. Post responses on flipchart, blackboard,
      or whiteboard.
      - What are their individual goals for participating in this
        project?
      - What are their collective goals for participating in this project?
      - What professional learning needs do they have?
      - What instructional strategies do they want to use? Do they
        need suggestions?
      - What background do they have in instructional technology?
      - What background do they have in learner-centered instruc-
        tion?

- • How can the developer serve as a resource to them?
  b. Provide validation of their goals. Indicate where certain goals will be met in other courses (e.g., advanced topics).
  c. Incorporate as many of their goals as possible in this workshop.
  d. Communicate which goals will be included in this workshop and which will hopefully be addressed in future classes.
3. Presentation of sample strategies to use in this assignment. The faculty discusses and chooses one or more.
  a. Project-based learning
  b. Small group discussions
  c. Collaborative writing
  d. Reflective journals
  e. Simulations
  f. Role-playing
  g. Case studies
  h. Critical incidents
  i. Online discussions
  j. Listservs

4. Facilitating the learning activities. This sample learning activity has the faculty learners selecting case study and small group work activities.
  a. Pose and clarify a selection of these initial critical questions.
    • What is a learner-centered classroom?
    • What does it look and sound like?
    • Who are my learners and what experience do they have in learner-centered classrooms?
    • What kind of learning am I most comfortable with?
    • In what ways would a learner-centered orientation benefit my learners?
  b. Discuss what additional critical questions the faculty would like to add.
  c. Clarify developer's role as facilitator and the faculty's roles as co-learners.
  d. Facilitate a small group assignment. Establish a timeline of one semester and goals described below.
    Excerpt from Chapter 3:
    . . . They decide on a project-based format and set as their project the integration of technology into the Russian Studies curriculum. In so doing the professors divide up areas and tasks to de-

velop the details of the revision . . . Some do fact-finding research about educational technology in their content area, others research the changing accreditation standards, others contact colleagues to determine what programs in other colleges are doing, and another group consults with colleagues on campus to determine resources and strategies already available and being used. As the professors gather each week to report on their progress, they focus on the "what" of their learning, the content, but they also discuss the reflective teaching and learning journals they are keeping.

   e. Visit the groups, providing limited input.
- Encourage the faculty to use their experience, understanding and research to resolve differences and find answers.
- Encourage the faculty to consider multiple perspectives of different educational philosophies.
- Encourage faculty to ask deeper questions of purpose, cost-benefit, obstacles, and dynamics of instructional technologies under consideration.
- Recommend where resources might be accessed.

   f. Observe and evaluate these key progress points.
- Discussion of their learning orientation
- Group development of reflective questions
- Group development of project format, goals, and time frame
- Small group progress on project
- Small group debriefing sessions
- Group presentations

5. Conclusion. Use small group presentations as a synthesizing activity.
   a. Facilitate group presentations which may include the following.
- Their draft and final curriculum
- Discussion of learning process, problems, issues, and realizations
- Discussion of unresolved questions and concerns
- Answers to questions from the other groups
- Development of topics for further study

   b. Large group synthesis of all of the group presentations (see evaluation questions).

6. Evaluation and follow-up
   a. Complete the faculty evaluation through observations of small groups and final products.

      i. Learning related to transformative learning
- Within this context, these faculty learners may find themselves questioning and analyzing their assumptions about teaching and learning, their preconceptions of roles in the classroom, and their self-understanding.
- How do they feel about being the center of learning in this professional development project?
- What are they learning about themselves as learners? Do they have certain preferences of learning, or particular dislikes? What do they value about teaching and learning?
- What do they want their learners to gain from their courses of study?
- What is their purpose in teaching their content areas?
- Do they want to adopt a learner-centered model for their classrooms? If so, where does it fit in appropriately and how do they go about introducing and implementing it?
- How can they continue to broaden their understanding and vision of teaching and learning through questioning educational and philosophical assumptions, new information, and controversies?
- Did they critically question, analyze information, seek out resources, and/or synthesize their views and understanding?

    ii. Content learning gains
- What benefits are there to this instructional technique and focus?
- What drawbacks and difficulties are they encountering?
- What strategies can they adopt for additional curriculum development?

  b. Complete the developer's evaluation, using your reflective journal and the learner feedback about facilitation needs and difficulties encountered.

7. Extension. Consider additional possibilities that faculty and developer may pursue.
  a. Individual or collaborative integrative essays.
  b. Collaborative reflective article or conference presentation about the curriculum development process and experience.
  c. Selection of the next development initiatives based on interest in the current topic and additional topics or needs that emerged.

     d. Development of faculty groups that would continue curriculum development.

8. Recommendations for further revisions
     a. Consider where problems arose and how to prevent them
     b. Review the questions the faculty had and improve ways to clarify the project from the beginning.
     c. Consider providing access to resources that were difficult for the faculty learners to access but were central to the project.
     d. Consider how the faculty members may maximize self-directed learning skills in this project.
     e. Explore possibilities to integrate more reflective practice into the workshop activities.
     f. Increase development of self-directed learning practices.
     g. Provide additional or alternative self-assessment tools.

APPENDIX G

Instructional Strategies and Resources

This compilation of instructional strategies' definitions, examples, and resources provides selected options for educators and learners. Certainly not an exhaustive list, it is intended to jumpstart discussions of possibilities. Chapter references in Resources refer to chapters in this book. Please refer to Chapter 2 to see how this appendix may be used effectively within the proposed model.

CASE STUDIES

Definition: Descriptive accounts of situations are presented to the learners in order for them to make critical observations, answer questions, or solve a problem.

Examples: Learners provide possible responses to customer service scenarios. Extended case study about reconciling family life and work responsibilities

Resources: Chapter 3; Brookfield (1998); King (2003a); Klein (1993); Marsick (1998).

CHATROOMS

Definition: Live online discussions where participants type in responses that immediately appear on the screen.

Examples: Class members meet online at a specific time to solve a case study about an immigrant to their host country. Learners meet online to ask questions of a professional who logs on from a distant city.

Resources: Chapter 3; Bauer (2002); King (2003a); Palloff & Pratt (2001).

COLLABORATIVE LEARNING

Definition: Groups of learners work as a team to accomplish a learning assignment.

Examples: Group determines methods and then conducts research about daily living conditions during a U.S. historical period. ABE learners assist one another in class assignments.

Resources: Chapter 3; Apps (1991); Eisen (2000); King (2003a); Peters & Armstrong (1998); Vella (2002).

COLLABORATIVE WRITING

Definition: Learners write an essay, paper, etc., together through several possible formats.

Examples: Online collaborative writing project regarding their respective countries of origin. Small group collaborative writing of group consensus regarding the interpretation of a specific reading.

Resources: Chapter 3; Clark & Watson (1998); Wilcox (1997).

CRITICAL INCIDENTS

Definition: A posed, problematic situation used as a basis for discussion and critique.

Examples: Personal response to a neighborhood racial integration scenario. Group discussion of responses to a biased personnel evaluation.

Resources: Chapter 3; Brookfield (1998).

DEBATE

Definition: Teams or individuals take opposing views, usually on a controversial topic, and discuss via points and counterpoints in front of an audience.

Examples: Debate on affirmative action in college admissions. Debate on economic consequences of military action.

Resources: Chapter 3; Apps (1991); Brookfield (1998).

DISCUSSION

Definition: Communication exchange among two or more participants to engage in many possible purposes including sharing different views, solving problems, or exploring ideas.

Examples: ABE learners discuss their reactions to current events and plan additional research for selected topics. College students share perspectives on why an author chose a specific setting for a novel.

Resources: Chapter 3; Brookfield (1998); Brookfield & Preskill (1999); Vella (2002).

DRAMA

Definition: Development and/or performance of a dramatic reading, scene, play, or musical selection to communicate learning.

Examples: Group presents a musical performance and interpretation to communicate renewed life vision. Group presents an original brief dramatic play of intercultural responses to grief.

Resources: Chapter 3; Gallagher (1997); Taylor (1998).

ESSAYS

Definition: Written submission on a selected topic (usually less formal and shorter than a term paper).

Examples: Essay on students' personal immigration experiences. Essay on diversity in the workplace.

Resources: Chapter 3; Gray (2002); Van Halen-Faber (1997).

FREQUENTLY ASKED QUESTIONS (FAQs)

Definition: A compilation of questions and answers on a specific topic that usually is posted on the Web.

Examples: Help files for learning a computer graphics programs. Catalog of questions and answers regarding visiting a specific country or city.

Resources: Chapter 5; King (2003a).

INTERVIEWS

Definition: Participants ask questions of an individual who is of particular interest to the class, maybe because of occupation, situation, etc.

Examples: ABE learners interview an office manager about job skills. ESOL learners interview a college admissions officer.

Resources: Chapter 3; Apps (1991); King (2003a).

JOURNALS

Definitions: Learners write accounts of their thoughts and experiences on specific topic.

Examples: Student journal of their cultural experiences or their travels. Learners journal daily about their group project experience and learning. Learners keep a reading journal regarding newspaper articles on a specific topic.

Resources: Chapter 3; Boud (2001); Hiemstra (2001); King (2003a).

LEARNING CONTRACTS

Definition: A written record of what the learner and teacher decide about what objectives, assignments, timeline, and/or evaluation will be pursued in a class, course, or program of study.

Examples: Learning contract for an ESOL learner preparing for the TOEFEL exam. A learning contract for assignments and evaluation in an advanced psychology class.

Resources: Chapter 1; Berger, Caffarella, & O'Donnell (2004); Brookfield & Preskill (1999).

LISTSERV

Definition: Discussion facilitated by an email distribution list. Participants sign up via a computer and when members send a message to the group, they all receive copies of it in their email boxes.

Examples: Faculty share technology integration tips. Adult learners sign up for a listserv that supports a GED preparation class.

Resources: Chapter 5; King (2003a); Palloff & Pratt (2001).

ONLINE DISCUSSION

Definition: Participants engage in discussion via an online forum. They go to a website and post answers, responses, or other comments. Other learners can later go read these and respond in turn.

Examples: Online classes use web-based, "threaded" (or themed) discussions to explore complex environmental engineering cases. Learners continue face-to-face class discussion about workplace ethics throughout the week online.

Resources: Chapter 3; King (2001, 2003a); Palloff & Pratt (2001); White & Bridwell (1998).

PORTFOLIOS

Definition: Collection of a learner's work that can demonstrate skill, knowledge, application, etc.

Examples: Art students' portfolios of sketches and paintings. Math students' portfolios of solved problems, exercises, and projects.

Resources: Chapter 3; Black et al. (1994).

READINGS

Definition: Assigned or selected material that relates to subject matter.

Examples: Using short stories, books, magazine articles, newspaper articles, Internet sites, and other publications that pique interest and support further research regarding political science.

Resources: Chapter 3; Brookfield (1998); King (2003a).

ROLE-PLAYING

Definition: Learners adopt different roles or characteristics in order to act out, practice, or troubleshoot a situation.

Examples: Practicing for job interviews. Adopting the role of a mother-in-law in parenting classes.

Resources: Chapter 4; Apps (1991); Vella (2002).

ROUND-ROBIN DISCUSSION OR CIRCLE OF VOICES

Definition: All participants sequentially offer their answers or perspectives in a group discussion.

Examples: Students, one by one, discuss their reactions to a problematic scenario regarding foreign policy. Learners take turns sharing their rationale for their solutions in a math word problem.

Resources: Chapter 3; Brookfield & Preskill (1999).

SIMULATIONS

Definition: Prefabricated close to real-life scenarios that learners participate in to practice or critically examine a specific situation.

Examples: Learning of office routines in a practice office environment. Web-based dissection of animals for a biology class.

Resources: Chapter 4; Gilley (1998); Klein (1993).

STUDENT PRESENTATIONS

Definition: Individuals or groups of students present the results of their research or other group work to an audience.

Examples: Presentations of warehouse renovation project. Group presentation of solutions to class scenarios regarding divergent historical perspectives of the Spanish-American War.

Resources: Chapter 3; Brookfield (1990).

TERM OR RESEARCH PAPERS

Definition: Organized written submission on a specific topic often based on student research.

Examples: Research on black American culture in the 1850s. Paper on integrating multiple perspectives of a world crisis.

Resources: Chapter 3; Coffin et al. (2003).

REFERENCES

Angelo, T., & Cross, K. P. (1998). *Classroom assessment techniques: A handbook for teachers.* (2nd ed.). San Francisco: Jossey-Bass.

Apps, J. (1991). *Mastering the teaching of adults.* Malabar, FL: Krieger.

Banta, T., Lund, J., Black, K., & Oblander, F. (1996). *Assessment in practice: Putting principles to work on college campuses.* San Francisco: Jossey-Bass.

Bauer, J. (1992). Assessing student work from chat rooms and bulletin boards. In R. Andersen, J. Bauer, and B. Speck (Eds.), *Assessment strategies for the on-line class; From theory to practice* (pp. 31-36). New Directions for Teaching and Learning, No. 91. San Francisco: Jossey-Bass.

Baumgartner, L. (2001). An update on transformative learning. In S. Merriam (Ed.), *The new update on adult learning theory* (pp. 15-24). New Directions for Adult and Continuing Education, No. 89. San Francisco: Jossey-Bass.

Belenky, M., Clinchy, B., Goldberger, N., & Tarule, J. (1996). *Women's ways of knowing* (2nd ed). New York: Basic Books.

Belenky, M., & Stanton, A. (2000). Inequality, development, and connected knowing. In. J. Mezirow and Associates (Eds.), *Learning as transformation* (pp. 71-102). San Francisco: Jossey-Bass.

Berger, N., Caffarella, R., & O'Donnell, J. (2004). Learning contracts. In M. Galbraith (Ed.), *Adult learning methods: A guide for effective instruction* (3rd ed.) (pp. 289-319). Malabar, FL: Krieger.

Black, L., Daiker, D., Sommers, J., & Stygall, G. (Eds.). (1994). *New directions in portfolio assessment.* Portsmouth, NH: Boyton/Cook Heinemann.

Boud, D. (2001). Using journal writing to enhance reflective practice. In L. English & M. Gillen (Eds.), *Promoting journal writing in adult education* (pp. 9-18). New Directions for Adult and Continuing Education, No. 90. San Francisco: Jossey-Bass.

195

Broad, R. (1994). 'Portfolio scoring': A contradiction in terms. In L. Black, D. Daiker, J. Sommers, & G. Stygall. (Eds.), *New directions in portfolio assessment* (pp. 263-276). Portsmouth, NH: Boyton/Cook Heinemann.

Brookfield, S. (1987). *Developing critical thinkers.* San Francisco: Jossey-Bass.

Brookfield, S. (1990). *The skillful teacher.* San Francisco: Jossey-Bass.

Brookfield, S. (1995). *Becoming a critically reflective teacher.* San Francisco: Jossey-Bass.

Brookfield, S. (2004). Discussion. In M. Galbraith (Ed.), *Adult learning methods: A guide for effective instruction* (3rd ed.) (pp. 209-226). Malabar, FL: Krieger.

Brookfield, S., & Preskill, S. (1999). *Discussion as a way of teaching.* San Francisco: Jossey-Bass.

Clark, M., & Watson, D. (1998). Women's experience of academic collaborations. In I. Saltiel, A. Sgroi, & R. Brockett (Eds.), *The power and potential of collaborative learning partnerships* (pp. 63-74). New Directions for Adult and Continuing Education, No. 79. San Francisco: Jossey-Bass.

Clark, M., & Wilson, A. (1991). Context and rationality in Mezirow's theory of transformational learning. *Adult Education Quarterly.* 41 (2), 75-91.

Coffin, C., Curry, M., Goodman, S., Hewings, A., Lilis, T., & Swann, J. (2003). *Teaching academic writing: A toolkit for higher education.* New York: Routledge.

Conti, G. (2004). Identifying your teaching style. In M. Galbraith (Ed.), *Adult learning methods: A guide for effective instruction* (3rd ed.) (pp. 75-91). Malabar, FL: Krieger.

Cornesky, R. (1993). *The quality professor: Implementing TQM in the classroom.* Madison, WI: Magna Publications.

Courts, P., & McInerney, K. (1993). *Assessment in higher education: Politics, pedagogy, and portfolios.* Westport, CT: Praeger.

Cranton, P. (1994). *Understanding and promoting transformative learning; A guide for educators of adults.* San Francisco: Jossey-Bass.

Cranton, P. (Ed.). (1997). *Transformative learning in action.* New Directions for Adult and Continuing Education, No. 74. San Francisco: Jossey-Bass.

Cranton, P. (1997). Preface. In P. Cranton (Ed.), *Transformative learning in action* (pp. 1-3). New Directions for Adult and Continuing Education, No. 74. San Francisco: Jossey-Bass.

Cranton, P. (2000). Individual differences and transformative learning.

In. J. Mezirow & Associates (Eds.). *Learning as transformation* (pp. 181-204). San Francisco: Jossey-Bass.

Cranton, P. (2001). *Becoming an authentic teacher in higher education.* Malabar, FL: Krieger.

Creswell, J. (2002). *Research design: Qualitative, quantitative and mixed methods.* Thousand Oaks, CA: Sage.

Creswell, J. (1998). *Qualitative inquiry and research design.* Thousand Oaks, CA: Sage.

Cross, K. P., & Angelo, T. (1988). *Classroom assessment techniques: A handbook for teachers.* San Francisco: Jossey-Bass.

Daloz, L. (1999). *Mentor: Guiding the journey of adult learning.* San Francisco: Jossey-Bass.

Daloz, L. (2000). Transformative learning for the common good. In J. Mezirow & Associates (Eds.), *Learning as transformation* (pp. 103-124). San Francisco: Jossey-Bass.

Dean, G. J. (2002). *Designing instruction for adult learners* (2nd ed.). Malabar, FL: Krieger.

Dirkx, J. (1997). Nurturing the soul in adult learning. In P. Cranton (Ed.), *Transformative learning in action.* New Directions for Adult and Continuing Education (pp. 79-88), No. 74. San Francisco: Jossey-Bass.

Eisen, M. (2000). The many faces of team teaching and learning: An overview. In M. Eisen, & L. Tisdell (Eds.), *Team teaching and learning in adult education* (pp. 5-14). New Directions for Adult and Continuing Education, No. 87, San Francisco: Jossey-Bass.

Elias, J., & Merriam, S. (1995). *Philosophical foundations of adult education* (2nd ed.). Malabar, FL: Krieger.

English, L. (2001). Ethical concerns relating to journal writing. In L. English & M. Gillen (Eds.), *Promoting journal writing in adult education* (pp. 27-36). New Directions for Adult and Continuing Education, No. 90. San Francisco: Jossey-Bass.

English, L., & Gillen, M. (Eds.) (2001) *Promoting journal, writing in adult education.* New Directions for Adult and Continuing Education, No 90. San Francisco: Jossey-Bass.

Fosnot, C. T. (1996). *Constructivism: Theory, perspectives, and practice.* New York: Teachers' College Press.

Gagne, R., Briggs, L., & Wager, W. (1992). *Principles of instructional design* (4th ed.). New York: Harcourt, Brace, & Jovanovich.

Galbraith, M. (2004). The teacher of adults. In M. Galbraith (Ed.), *Adult learning methods: A guide for effective instruction* (3rd ed.) (pp. 3-21). Malabar, FL: Krieger.

Gall, M.D., Borg, W. R., & Gall, J. P. (1996). *Educational resources: An introduction* (6ᵗʰ ed.) White Plains: Longman.

Gallagher, C. (1997). *Drama-in-education: Adult teaching and learning for change in understanding and practice.* Unpublished doctoral dissertation, University of Wisconsin.

Gilley, J. (2004). Demonstration and simulation In M. Galbraith (Ed.), *Adult learning methods: A guide for effective instruction* (3ʳᵈ ed.) (pp. 361-381). Malabar, FL: Krieger.

Grabove, S. (1997). The many facets of transformative learning theory and practice. In P. Cranton (Ed.), *Transformative learning in action* (pp. 89-96). New Directions for Adult and Continuing Education, No. 74. San Francisco: Jossey-Bass.

Gray, R. (2002). Assessing students' written projects. In R. Andersen, J. Bauer, & B. Speck (Eds.), *Assessment strategies for the on-line class; From theory to practice* (pp. 37-42). New Directions for Teaching and Learning, No. 91. San Francisco: Jossey-Bass.

Hiemstra, R. (2001). Uses and benefits of journal writing. In L. English & M. Gillen (Eds.), *Promoting journal writing in adult education* (pp. 19-26). New Directions for Adult and Continuing Education, No. 90. San Francisco: Jossey-Bass.

Kegan, R. (1994). *In over our heads: The mental demands of modern life.* Cambridge, MA: Harvard University Press.

Kegan, R. (2001). What 'Form' transforms? A constructive-developmental approach to transformative learning. In. J. Mezirow & Associates (Eds.), *Learning as transformation* (pp. 35-70). San Francisco: Jossey-Bass.

King, K. P. (1997). Examining learning activities and transformative learning. *International Journal of University Adult Education*, 36 (3), 23-37.

King, K. P. (2000). The adult ESL experience: Facilitating perspective transformation in the classroom. *Adult Basic Education: An Interdisciplinary Journal for Adult Literacy Educators*, 10 (2), 69-89.

King, K. P. (2001). Educators revitalize the classroom 'Bulletin Board': A case study of the influence of online dialogue on face-to-face classes from an adult learning perspective. *Journal of Research on Computing in Education*, 33(4), 337-354.

King, K. P. (2002). *Keeping pace with technology: Educational technology that transforms. Vol. 1: The challenge and promise for K-12 educators.* Cresskill, NJ: Hampton Press.

King, K. P. (2003a). *Keeping pace with technology: Educational technology that transforms. Vol. 2: The challenge and promise for higher edu-*

cation faculty. Cresskill, NJ: Hampton Press.

King, K. P. (2003b). Understanding adult learners amidst societal crisis: Learning and grief in tandem. *The Journal of Continuing Higher Education,* 5 (20), 13-25.

King, K. P. (2003/2001). The tail of the comet: Helping faculty focus on their pathway of discovery in learning and using technology. *Journal of Faculty Development,* 18 (4), 123-130.

King, K. P. (2004a). Both sides now: Examining transformational learning professional development experience, practice, and accountability. *Innovative Higher Education,* 29 (2), 153-172.

King, K. P. (2004b). Exploring critical pedagogy in the shadow of tragedy. *Radical Pedagogy* 5 (2).

King, K. P., Bennett, J., Perrera, G., & Matewa, M. (2003). An international interpretation from Ground Zero. In D. Flowers, M. Lee, A. Schelstrate, & V. Sheared (Eds.). *Proceedings of the 44th Annual Adult Education Research Conference* (pp. 241-246). San Francisco: San Francisco State University.

King, K. P., & Jakuta, M. A. (2002). Needs assessment recommendations for practice from the field: A case study. *Adult Basic Education: An Interdisciplinary Journal for Adult Literacy Educators,* 12 (3), 157-172.

King, K. P., & Lawler, P. A. (2003). Best practices in faculty development in North American higher education: Distinctions and dilemmas. *Journal of Faculty Development,* 19(1) 29-36.

King, K. P., & Wright, L. (2003). New perspectives on gains in the ABE classroom: Transformative learning results considered. *Adult Basic Education: An Interdisciplinary Journal for Adult Literacy Educators,* 13(2) 100-123.

LaCava, D. (2002). *Perspective transformation in adult ESL learners using internet technology.* Unpublished doctoral dissertation, Department of Education, Fordham University.

Lawler, P. A., & King, K. P. (2000). *Preparing for effective faculty development: Using adult learning strategies.* Malabar, FL: Krieger.

Magro, K. (2002). Exploring teaching roles and responsibilities in adult literacy education. *Perspectives: The New York Journal of Adult Learning,* 1(1), 21-33.

Marsick, V. (2004). Case study. In M. Galbraith (Ed.), *Adult learning methods: A guide for effective instruction* (3rd ed.) (pp. 383-404). Malabar, FL: Krieger.

Merriam, S., & Caffarella, R. (1999). *Learning in adulthood* (2nd ed.). San Francisco: Jossey-Bass.

Mezirow, J. (1978). *Education for perspective transformation; Women's re-entry programs in community colleges.* New York: Teacher's College, Columbia University.

Mezirow, J. (1991). *Transformative dimensions of adult learning.* San Francisco: Jossey-Bass.

Mezirow, J. (1997). Transformative learning: Theory to practice. In P. Cranton (Ed.), *Transformative learning in action* (pp. 5-12). New Directions for Adult and Continuing Education, No. 74. San Francisco: Jossey-Bass.

Mezirow, J., & Associates (1990). *Fostering critical reflection in adulthood; A guide to transformative and emancipatory learning.* San Francisco: Jossey-Bass.

Mezirow J., & Associates (Eds.) (2000). *Learning as transformation.* San Francisco: Jossey-Bass.

Miller, A., Imrie, B., & Cox, K. (1998). *Student assessment in higher education.* London: Kogan Page.

Mills, G. (2000). *Action research: A guide for the teacher researcher.* Upper Saddle River, NJ: Prentice-Merrill.

Morse, J. M., & Richards, M. (2002). *Readme first for a user's guide to qualitative methods.* Thousand Oaks: Sage.

Nardi, P. M. (2003). *Doing survey research: A guide to quantitative methods.* Boston: Allyn and Bacon.

O'Sullivan, E., Morrell, A., & O'Connor, M. (2002). *Exploring the boundaries of transformative learning.* New York: Palgrave.

Palloff, R., & Pratt, K. (2001). *Lessons from the cyberspace classroom: The realities of online teaching.* San Francisco: Jossey-Bass.

Palmer, P. (1998). *The courage to teach: Exploring the inner landscape of a teacher's life.* San Francisco: Jossey-Bass.

Palomba, C., & Banta, T. (1999). *Assessment essentials.* San Francisco: Jossey-Bass.

Peters, J., & Armstrong, J. (1998). Collaborative learning: People laboring together to construct knowledge. In I. Saltiel, A. Sgroi, & R. Brockett (Eds.), *The power and potential of collaborative learning partnerships* (pp.75-86). New Directions for Adult and Continuing Education, No. 79. San Francisco: Jossey-Bass.

Pilling-Cormick, J. (1997). Transformative and self-directed learning in practice. In P. Cranton (Ed.), *Transformative learning in action* (pp. 69-78). New Directions for Adult and Continuing Education, No. 74. San Francisco: Jossey-Bass.

Pratt, D. (1998). *Five perspectives of teaching in adult and higher edu-*

cation. Malabar, FL: Krieger.

Queeney, D. (1995). *Assessing needs in continuing education.* San Francisco: Jossey-Bass.

Quigley, B. A., & Norton, M. (2003). 'It simple makes us better': Literacy research-in-practice in the U.S., Britain, Australia, and Canada. *Perspectives: The New York Journal of Adult Learning,* 1(2), 5-17.

Sax, G. (1989). *Principles of educational and psychological measurement and evaluation* (3rd ed.). Belmont, CA: Wadsworth.

Schön, D. (1987). *Educating the reflective practitioner.* San Francisco: Jossey-Bass.

Senge, P. (1990). *The fifth discipline: The art and practice of the learning organization.* New York: Doubleday.

Taylor, E. (1998). *The theory and practice of transformative learning: A critical review, information series No. 374.* Columbus, OH: ERIC Clearing House on Adult, Career, and Vocational Education.

Taylor, E. (2000a). Analyzing research on transformative learning theory. In. J. Mezirow and Associates (Eds.), *Learning as transformation* (pp. 285-328). San Francisco: Jossey-Bass.

Taylor, E. (2000b). Fostering Mezirow's transformative learning theory in the adult education classroom: A critical review. *The Canadian Journal for the Study of Adult Education,* 14(2), 1-28.

Thomas, A. (2000). Prior learning assessment: The quiet revolution. In A. Wilson & E. Hayes (Eds.), *Handbook of adult and continuing education* (New ed.). San Francisco: Jossey-Bass.

Van Halen-Faber, C. (1997). Encouraging critical reflection in teacher education. In P. Cranton (Ed.), *Transformative learning in action: Insights from practice* (pp. 51-60). New Directions for Adult and Continuing Education, No. 74. San Francisco: Jossey-Bass.

Vella, J. (2002). *Learning to listen, learning to teach.* San Francisco: Jossey-Bass.

White, B., & Bridwell, C. (2004). Distance learning techniques. In M. Galbraith (Ed.). *Adult learning methods: A guide for effective instruction* (3rd ed.) (pp. 273-288). Malabar, FL: Krieger.

White, E. (1994). Portfolios as an assessment concept. In L. Black, D. Daiker, J. Sommers, & G. Stygall (Eds.), *New directions in portfolio assessment* (pp. 25-39). Portsmouth, NH: Boyton/Cook Heinemann.

Wilcox, S. (1997). Becoming a faculty developer. In P. Cranton (Ed.), *Transformative learning in action: Insights from practice* (pp. 23-32). New Directions for Adult and Continuing Education, No. 74. San Francisco: Jossey-Bass.

Wiessner, C., & Mezirow, J. (2000). Theory building and the search for common ground. In J. Mezirow & Associates (Eds.), *Learning as transformation* (pp. 329-358). San Francisco: Jossey-Bass.

Yin, R. K. (2003). *Case study research: Design and methods* (3rd ed.). Thousand Oaks, CA: Sage.

Zinn, L. (2004). Exploring your philosophical orientation. In M. Galbraith (Ed.), *Adult learning methods: A guide for effective instruction* (3rd ed.) (pp. 39-74). Malabar, FL: Krieger.

INDEX